THE **EBONY** EXODUS PROJECT

THE EBONY EXODUS PROJECT

Why Some Black Women Are Walking
Out on Religion—and Others Should Too

Candace R. M. Gorham, LPC

PITCHSTONE PUBLISHING
DURHAM, NORTH CAROLINA

Pitchstone Publishing
Durham, NC 27705
www.pitchstonepublishing.com

To contact the publisher, please e-mail info@pitchstonepublishing.com

Printed in the United States of America

19 18 17 16 15 14 13   1 2 3 4 5

Library of Congress Cataloging-in-Publication Data

Gorham, Candace R. M.
 The ebony exodus project : why some Black women are walking out on religion—and others should too / Candace R.M. Gorham, LPC.
    pages cm
 Includes bibliographical references and index.
 ISBN 978-1-939578-02-0 (pbk. : alk. paper)
1. African American women—Religion. 2. African American churches. 3. African American women—Social conditions. 4. African American women—Economic conditions. 5. African American women—Mental health. I. Title.
 BR563.N4G675 2013
 277.3'083082—dc23
                             2013015333

CONTENTS

To Tamahl
for saying,
"Just start."

PREFACE

When people ask me about my reasons for starting the Ebony Exodus Project (www.EbonyExodus.com)—a forum for black women who are thinking about leaving organized religion or who have already left it behind—my response is always the same: *black women are the single most religious demographic in the United States, yet they are at the bottom of the totem pole in practically every measure of quality of life—physical health, financial health, mental health, and more.*

If the Black Church wants to take credit for all of the good things that happen in the lives of black women, it must also take some of the blame for all of the bad things. You might get tired of hearing this refrain throughout this book, which is an extension of the broader Ebony Exodus Project, because I will repeat it. If readers walk away from this book with an increased awareness of one thing, my hope is that it will be the message contained in the italicized statement above.

I was one of those devout black women who really, *really* believed. From the age of five or six, I always believed. I was sure that god was going to bestow upon me all of the blessings the Bible speaks of precisely because I was a "true" believer who gave my all to god. So, I grew up to be an ordained minister—and a "statistic" regarding my physical health, my financial health, and, not least of which, my mental health.

As early as age eight or nine, I started displaying signs of mood disturbances, and by early adulthood, they were becoming debilitating. But everyone—all of my friends, family, pastors, and fellow church members—told me that I absolutely was not depressed, that I wasn't "crazy," and that I shouldn't even "think like that" because I was such a strong woman.

I understand now that depression definitely runs in my family, but no one in my family saw depression for what it was, so all I could do was to try to bury my angst. And that's what I did—for years. My peers and elders at the church only amplified this pattern of denial. Indeed, regardless of whether a person is dealing with depression because of chronic environmental stressors or because of genetics, the church often does not acknowledge how serious a disease depression can be. By the time I had my daughter, the symptoms—the suicidality, the anger, the anxiety, the hopelessness—had become too dangerous to ignore.

I took the frightening steps of seeking secular counseling and taking medication. In addition to the depression and anxiety that was ruining my life, I was morbidly obese. I prayed and tried to depend on god to help me lose weight. But the church to which I belonged did not do anything to help. There was little education on physical health in the church, and more problematically, my involvement with the church did not leave me time to take care of my physical self. I was busy nearly every day of the week attending services, delivering messages, conducting outreach, attending ministerial meetings, cleaning the building, and, oh yeah, attending more services.

At the age of twenty-one, I was ordained as an evangelist. Shortly thereafter I was ordained as an eldress and prophetess. With these positions, I was required to provide street ministry, preach messages, conduct home visits, and pray for church members. And I jumped in, full of gusto and zeal for the lord.

After a while, the belief that Jesus is all we need in the world began to lose its power of persuasion. The reason was simple: I educated myself. My story is not unique. As you will hear throughout this book, many ex-religious women—myself included—believe that education is the most important step a woman can take to free herself from the bonds of religion. I'm not talking only about formal education, although that helps, too. For me, a combination of both formal and informal education put me on the path away from religious belief.

The journey began, ironically enough, when I decided to study my religion in depth precisely because I was having so many troubles in my life—foreclosure, sickness, poverty. I truly believed that god had the answer for me, but that I must have been doing something wrong.

At the same time, I entered a graduate-level counseling program, which increased my sense of empathy, both toward myself and toward others whom I had always judged. In turn, I became more open to views I'd always found suspect—including views that ran completely counter to what I myself had been actively preaching. Thus, as my studies progressed and I started to see, for example, that there were problems with the translation and interpretation of the Bible, my world was officially knocked off of its axis.

Through a long, slow, painful, and frightening process of over two years, I moved through stages of being an unaffiliated believer, to being a non-Christian theist, to being an agnostic, to finally being an atheist. Facebook and YouTube became my best friends as I interacted with other nonbelievers and watched religious debates. In addition to being exposed to the big names of the "new atheist" movement, I was also exposed to a whole new world of freethinkers, skeptics, and atheists. Of course, the most exciting find, for me, was groups of black nonbelievers and atheists. I had no idea that such a community existed.

Even today, I continue to struggle with talking to my old friends and family about my atheism. While many of the people close to me know that I disdain church and religion, I've never actually told any of them that I'm an "atheist," save two or three. To some, I've said, "I'm agnostic." To others, I've said, "I really don't care anymore."

I imagine that many of them have put two and two together simply by browsing my Facebook page, but I'm trying to start using the word "atheist" more. At the very moment that I am typing these words, I worry about how many of my relationships will be strained or end completely after this book is published.

Despite how heavy-laden the word "atheist" is, I feel so strongly about the topic and I care so much about the well-being of black women that I just had to follow my heart and write this book.

A Note about Labels and Self-identification

The following are important terms you will see in this book related to self-identity. It is important to recognize that, while these terms are not mutually exclusive, they do all have distinct meanings, and individuals have various reasons for accepting or rejecting certain terms in describing their identity and world view.

Atheist—the lack of a belief in a god. It's important to note that this does not mean that a person professes to know that there is not a god.

Agnostic—literally, without knowledge. Agnostics typically believe that we do not have enough knowledge to say whether there is or is not a god.

Freethinker—a person who forms his or her beliefs and opinions independent of authority or dogma.

Nontheist/Nonbeliever—These terms are essentially interchangeable with atheist. However, some people prefer these terms because they do not have as strong as a negative connotation as "atheist."

Skeptic—a person who uses rational inquiry to evaluate claims. Skeptics demand convincing evidence and believe that all claims should undergo intense scrutiny, especially with the use of the scientific method when possible.

Humanist—a person who believes that we should focus our energy and efforts on improving life for humanity without dependence on a supernatural entity. Humanists are not always atheists. This is more of a philosophical stance than a spiritual declaration. Many atheists endorse secular humanism as a fully formed moral system that is not based on holy books and belief in gods.

Secularist—a person who believes that religion and religious beliefs should be separated from civil and governmental affairs.

Antitheist—one who actively and strongly opposes religion of all kinds.

A Note about the Interviews and Research Methods

The narratives you will read all come from interviews that I conducted between January and August 2011, when I put out a call through social media for black women who were willing to share their stories with me about their journeys away from religion. For those women who wished to have their identities protected, I have changed names and other identifying information for purposes of privacy. I have also changed certain names and details to protect the identities of people referred to in the stories. As some of the interviews were quite lengthy, I am able to share only those passages that are most relevant to the topic under discussion. I do, however, try to provide relevant context for each of the interviews. Aside from changes made for purposes of privacy and length, and some minor adjustments made for purposes of clarity, the words of the women are presented exactly as I heard them. My hope is that the reader can hear their unique voices just as I did.

One final note: all Bible scripture quoted in the book is from the King James Version unless otherwise noted.

A Note About the Interviews and Research Method

"The history of progress is written in the blood of men and women who have dared to espouse an unpopular cause, as, for instance, the black man's right to his body, or woman's right to her soul."

—Emma Goldman

INTRODUCTION

"Am I therefore become your enemy, because I tell you the truth?"
—*Galatians 4:16*

I am sure that plenty of people will have a lot to say about me and this book. I hope to hear more good than bad, but I anticipate a lot of push back and criticism for a number of reasons. For one, as the "new atheist" movement (as some call it) grows stronger, the Religious Right is becoming more vocal about how America is going to hell in a handbasket for tolerating people like me. This book will be seen as just another manifestation of America's growing "godless problem." But I expect that the angriest responses will come from the very black women toward whom this book is principally directed. Many of them will be shocked and disgusted, and I can hear the choruses now.

Criticism #1: "You obviously hate black women and therefore you hate yourself. This book is really about hatred."

If you read this book carefully and do not get caught up in the provocative title, you will see that I give a very empathetic analysis of the plight of black women. I am a proud black woman who has experienced firsthand many of the issues discussed in this book. I do not judge those who are struggling with the very things with which I struggled also. This book is not about hatred. It is about shining a light in a dark place. It is about exposing some of the shameful and embarrassing things that go on in black homes and churches that are either ignored by the leaders or explicitly sanctioned by the doctrines—terrible things such as sexual and physical abuse in the name of marriage submission, corporal punishment to instill morals into the children, and self-debasement as a way to demonstrate one's humility.

Often, black women say that they do not talk about some of these issues because they have a peaceful assurance that god is working everything out for their good. They point to prophecies and "words" from the lord regarding many of these embarrassing issues and, since they have that assurance, they believe there's no need to rehash these issues over and over—or to be proactive about solving their problems. The biggest problem with this logic is that things often do not get better or, if things do improve, the women fail to give credit where credit is due, such as to themselves or others. Such faith and confidence is not doing much beyond the expected placebo effect to help. This book is meant to start a new kind of conversation about the truth of what is going on with black women. It is a hopeful but honest book.

Criticism #2: "You're blaming all of the ills in the black community on black churches. That's a simple, shortsighted, narrow-minded view that doesn't take into account racism, poverty, or oppression by white people."

I admit that on the surface this book seems to be blaming all of the evils in the world on black churches. I also understand that, when taking on a topic as big and broad as the plight of black women, there will be no simple answers. There are a myriad of road blocks, difficulties, and hardships that black women endure and overcome daily, and not all of them are connected to black churches. A section of a library could easily be filled addressing each of these very important issues. For this book, I am focusing on only one thing, the contributing factors of the Black Church to the plight of black women today. Most people have no problem praising the Black Church and crediting it with all of the progress in the black community. Everyone likes to credit the entire Civil Rights Movement to the Black Church. Everyone likes to praise black churches for the charitable work they do providing food or helping people get off drugs. Everyone reveres the strong black matriarch at the head of every family who does it all "in the strength of the lord."

So, if the Black Church gets all the credit, it also has to take some of the blame. As Sikivu Hutchinson, author of *Moral Combat: Black Atheists, Gender Politics, and the Values War*, says, "When such factors as residential patterns, income levels, health outcomes, educational outcomes, incarceration rates, and transportation access are evaluated collectively, African-Americans experience the greatest disparities of any racial 'subgroup' in the US."[1]

Simply put: the black church cannot take *all* of the credit for the good unless it is willing to accept *all* the blame for the bad. Again, this is about shining a light in a dark place. This is about highlighting the ways in which religious, black-and-white, holier-than-thou thinking has damaged people. Sure, we could talk about how these exact problems also arise in white churches, in Judaism and Islam, and in most every other religion, but it is my belief that religion, in general, is oppressive, and I can focus only on one topic at a time. Has the Black Church ruined everything? No. Is the Black Church to blame for all the troubles in black communities? No. Does the Black Church share a large part of the responsibility for the problems and the lack of adequate responses to those problems? Yes. Should black churches and communities take a long hard look at themselves to make right their wrongs? Yes. As C. Eric Lincoln notes,

> To understand the power of the Black Church it must first be understood that there is no disjunction between the Black Church and the Black community. The church is the spiritual face of the Black community, and whether one is a "church member" or not is beside the point in any assessment of the importance and meaning of the Black Church. . . . The Black Church, then, is in some sense a "universal church," claiming and representing all Blacks. . . . The church still

accepts a broad-gauge responsibility for the Black community inside and outside its formal communion."[2]

And the only way to start a true healing process is to engage in an open, honest analysis and critique of such a powerful force as the Black Church.

Criticism #3: "Atheists are hateful people. They've only turned from god out of anger because they couldn't get everything they wanted from god. This book is simply the angry rants of pitiful people."

While I do not want this book to become a polemic about atheism and other forms of nonbelief, I believe that this anticipated critique is worth responding to. Believers who respond this way often do so because they are not listening to what the ex-religious have to say about themselves. Most atheists and nonbelievers who were previously religious came to their decision to leave religion as a result of their own consideration and study. In fact, most atheists who were raised in some sort of religion generally went through a slow, gradual, and often painful process of losing their religion. Usually, the "deconversion" process starts when a person has questions to which they cannot find satisfactory answers: What will happen to a child who dies before she is old enough to accept Jesus as savior? How is it fair that a ninety-year-old murderer who lived a terrible life can get to heaven just by asking for forgiveness with her dying breath while a kindhearted philanthropic Buddhist will end up in a hell for all of eternity? Why are there dinosaur bones if the Bible implies that the Earth is only six thousand years old? How did Adam and Eve populate the entire planet on their own?

Sometimes these questions lead a person to conclude that a fair and just god would not do certain things. At other times, the conflicts and contradictions become too many for the person to justify her continued belief. Or the person may decide that she still believes in god but does not adhere to a particular doctrine. Some of the deconversions in this book were grueling and agonizing, while others were quick epiphanies that occurred seemingly in an instant.

The point is that most atheists are not damaged goods who have left faith out of anger and frustration. They have likely left after careful study of the facts. While feeling hurt or empty might have started the search that ultimately ended in atheism, atheists report some of the highest rates of happiness and sense of purpose and freedom. This book is not an angry rant. It is about the need for women to constantly self-reflect and evaluate their lives.

Criticism #4: "There aren't many black atheists, agnostics, and nonbelievers. This book does not have an audience. So, it is irrelevant."

There are currently more atheists, agnostics, and nonbelievers in the United States than there are black people. Studies estimate that atheists make up approximately 15 percent of the population. The estimates go as high as 25 percent when you include descriptors like "nonbeliever," "agnostic," "unaffiliated," and "none." Since black people make up about 13 percent of the population, it stands to reason that there are a significant number of black nonbelievers who just have not "come out" as such.

Black nonbelievers who are already out hope that the number of out nonbelievers will reach a critical mass soon. When that tipping point is reached, there will likely be an outpouring of nonbelievers of all racial and ethnic backgrounds, especially black Americans. A similar thing happened with the gay rights movement in recent decades. As more and more gays and lesbians came out, those who were in the closet gained strength, confidence, motivation, and social support. They were able to see that they were not alone. Although there are still more rights to fight for related to sexual orientation, being gay has gradually become socially acceptable across much of the United States. As people realized that they knew amazing people who turned out to be closeted gays, they had no choice but to begin to admit that homosexuality is okay. The prediction is that the same thing will happen for nonbelievers, especially for black nonbelievers.

Hutchinson makes the point that, "While critics of the Black Church abound, few with an avowedly atheist or humanist sensibility, who question the basic relevance of all regimes of organized religion to black identity, black socioeconomic sustainability and social justice, have achieved mainstream visibility."[3] This book is a step in that direction. It speaks directly to black people about the uniquely intense effect that the Black Church has on black women. More importantly, this book aspires to reach out to those women and to foster an open dialogue. Hopefully, black women who want to shake off the bonds of religion will find the strength to do so.

Criticism #5: "What do you mean by 'The Black Church'? There is too much diversity in black churches to try to stereotype them and lump them all into one category."

This is true and it is impossible to speak clearly to all black women and to speak about all black churches. However, there is a general sense that Christianity in the black community has a different flavor than in white communities or in other racial and ethnic communities. Note scholars C. Eric Lincoln and Lawrence H. Mamiya, "The assumption that black churches constituted the central institutional sector in black communities is common in the American understanding of the black subculture. Reliable investigators have consistently underscored the fact that black churches were one of the few stable and coherent institutions to emerge from slavery."[4] Because of the shared past of slavery and the turmoil of the Civil Rights Movement, it is undeniable that there are significant cultural, behavioral, and social similarities and beliefs that connect all black Americans. So, while it would never be my intent to stereotype or lump all black people into one category, this book attempts to speak to some of those known and experienced similarities and that unspoken bond that many black Americans feel toward one another. There may be portions of this book that only speak to a small minority of black women, while there may be other portions that resonate with almost everyone.

—§—

Throughout the book, I attempt to be fair and acknowledge the fact that not all points in the book will apply to all people. However, it is also important to recognize that the personal stories are just that, the individual experiences of the women whose stories appear here. This book consists of the deeply personal and profound experiences of women who were more than excited and honored to share their stories with someone. Over the course of about six months, I conducted more than twenty recorded interviews and received several written interviews. While I wish that I could share all of the stories with you, I felt that the book would have a greater impact if it presented more well-rounded and fuller experiences as opposed to abbreviated snapshots. I attempted to ascertain similar information from all of the women. I asked all of them questions about their childhood experiences with religion, when and why their beliefs started to change, what impact they believe religion has on mental and physical health, and what they believe are some of the biggest problems facing the black community, particularly as they relate to the Black Church.

Part of the problem is evident in the simple fact that some of the women I interviewed requested that I use a pseudonym in the place of their real names because of the potential for backlash from their families, employers, and communities. To provide further anonymity to them, I either did not include or changed other potentially identifying information, such as cities, locations, or church names. I also conducted interviews with several prominent, up-and-coming leaders in the black atheist community, which is growing and beginning to flourish in parts of the United States. They did not ask me to change identifying facts, and you may just recognize some of them.

The book also contains six chapters on various topics interspersed between the personal stories. These topics address religion's effect on the black community in terms of mental and emotional health, physical health, sex, and the flawed thinking patterns that have allowed religion to become so firmly rooted in the black community. These chapters present facts and findings of scholarly research as well as the musings of other writers on these topics. But you must know that such research and such writings were hard to come by. There are shelves upon shelves of books that exhort women to submit to god and that supposedly share some divine wisdom that had been imparted to the author. But look on those same shelves, in the same religion sections of bookstores and libraries, and you will be hard pressed to find even one or two books that take the opposite stance. Even among academics, the negative effects of religion on the black community and, more specifically, on black women is not well researched.

As the purpose of this book is not to idly complain but to empower, in the concluding chapter I attempt to offer some solutions. As a counselor and mental health professional, it is my job to not only give people a safe space to vent, complain, and process emotions, but also to challenge them to grow, to see the world from other perspectives, and to discover what it is they need to do for themselves to improve their overall health and happiness. So is my goal with this book. And to that end I suggest things people can do for themselves, their families, and their communities in order to advance the positive effects that freethought can have on a person's life.

The impetus for this book is that, hopefully, it will make more black people think critically about their religious and supernatural beliefs and how the Black Church has negatively impacted their lives. The book is not about forcing atheism or nonbelief on others but about encouraging critical thinking and freethought. Instead of shutting down a conversation that is too lofty or contrary to long-held beliefs, the goal is to animate people to open their minds to new information or new points of view that they have probably never considered. Religious people often accuse nonreligious people of being close-minded. However, the very nature of "I'm-right-and-you're-wrong" belief systems requires the adherent to be close-minded. Ex-believers report that the difficulty in talking to friends and family about their nonbelief ranges from fleeting disinterest to heartbreaking ends.

Curious and doubting Christians can also become victims of the same kind of religious vitriol experienced by Anthony Burnside, a black man raised in a Pentecostal family who eventually sought meaning in New Age philosophies and the Nation of Islam before discovering secular humanism. About his experience, he says, "I started questioning everything with the same fervor I had as a Christian. I was ridiculed, insulted, and called Satan's child simply for questioning the Scriptures."[5] However, the difference between the experiences between most ex-believers and current believers is that the ex-religious person had to study or consider something new to change his or her beliefs. The ex-religious person had to be open-minded and to think critically.

As Hutchinson points out, "There has been scant serious evaluation of the perceived gendered social benefits of religious observance versus the social costs of being an atheist. In addition, there is virtually no critical literature assessing the implications of the issue for American women of color."[6] That is why I hope that religious black female readers—and, in truth, all readers—will find some similarities between the women whose stories are offered in this book and themselves. When reading the stories of the women who were brave enough to share their stories, the believer will discover similarities to their own stories and will hopefully be less judgmental of atheists and nonbelievers. I also hope that nonbelieving black women will find some comfort in these stories and shared experiences.

It is very difficult for black nonbelievers to come out of the closet because, "In the moral universe of mainstream African American communities, essentialism dictates that those who violate the tacit contract of religious observance are somehow 'less' than African American."[7] However, I hope that the nonreligious black community will be able to find increasing acceptance within the broader community, as this book and others like it create greater visibility for the larger African-American community. Despite the fact that "alternative belief systems are viewed with suspicion because they are 'inconsistent' with authentic black identity,"[8] I believe that this book will challenge some aspects of long-held religious and superstitious beliefs and encourage readers to be more curious and to analyze their beliefs.

I think that the black community as a whole needs to strive for a deeper, more meaningful conversation about the real impact and relevance of the Black Church today.

1

ON RELIGION
IN THE BLACK COMMUNITY

"Not Forsaking the Assembling of Ourselves Together."
—*Hebrews 10:25*

Drive through any black neighborhood and you are guaranteed to see churches on every corner. You will see signs advertising Christian daycares, Christian beauty salons, and Christian restaurants. Scripture verses pop up in some of the most unlikely places—like on restaurant signs and school yards. Crosses are everywhere.

Statistical studies bear this out. According to the 2008 American Religious Identification Survey, 86 percent of black people identify with some Christian denomination. The level of religiosity in the black community is also high, especially among black women. The 2008 Pew Forum on Religion and Public Life reports that more than eight in ten black women (84 percent) say religion is very important to them and that roughly six in ten (59 percent) say they attend religious services at least once a week.[1]

Black people love their religion even when they do not go to church. I used to be a street evangelist who went to some of the toughest neighborhoods in the cities in which I lived. It was not unusual to be invited into a home to talk and to find myself sitting beside people smoking marijuana, admitting that they did not go to church as much as they "should." In one instance, a person with whom I was speaking pointed to a large heirloom Bible that lay out on the coffee table opened to the 23rd Psalm: "The lord is my shepherd. I shall not want. . ."

A lot of observers attribute the pervasiveness of this level of religiosty in the black community to slavery. And truthfully a comprehensive discussion of black religiosity would not be complete without exploring this history. It is widely accepted that religion has, at various times and in some instances, been used as a tool to manipulate and control. Indeed, the Black Church began under duress, on pain of death and eternal damnation. But some black people have gone so far as to profess their gratitude for slavery because it introduced their ancestors to Jesus and paved the way for their own salvation. Without slavery, the thinking goes, they would have been born into a pagan tribe and doomed to spend all eternity in hell, even though they never would have even heard of Jesus. Of course, this line of reasoning is extremely faulty for a number of reasons (not to mention indicative of a cruel deity), not least of which because today many African countries are among the most Christian in the world.

Since slave masters told slaves how good their god was, is it any surprise that slaves, a lot of whom believed in the existence of many gods and spirits, would want to see if the slave masters' god would help them, too? The slaves' commitment to their new religion further solidified as the abolitionist movement got under way, when many religious leaders joined the fight. After all, it was their god, the god of Moses, who would lead them out of captivity into Canaan Land. Unfortunately, the slaves had forgotten, after decades of indoctrination and biblical censoring, that it was their new god who had enslaved them in the first place, the same way that Yahweh had allowed the enslavement of the Jews in Egypt. As Lincoln and Mamiya write, "The black church has often experienced difficulty in conceptualizing or knowing itself except as an amorphous, lusterless detail on some larger canvas devoted to other interests. In consequence the black church has often found itself repeating history it had already experienced, and relearning lessons it had long since forgotten."[2]

What people do not realize—including most in the black community—is that the abolitionist movement was largely initiated and supported by freethinkers. Sojourner Truth, for example, was relatively more freethinking than many know. Frederick Douglass was an atheist who was very vocal about his disdain for religion: "I would say welcome infidelity! Welcome atheism! Welcome anything! in preference to the gospel as preached by those divines [i.e., clergy who defend slavery]! They convert the very name of religion into a barbarous cruelty."[3]

The same is true for the Civil Rights Movement. Many people do not know the influential role black nonbelievers played in it. Although black religious leaders like Martin Luther King Jr. are often credited with the success of this movement, history has written out freethinkers and atheists like James Forman, A. Philip Randolph, James Baldwin, and Lorraine Hansberry. Often not remembered too is that much of the opposition to the movement in white America came from church folk who found support for their hatred in the Bible. In their opinions—and according to the Bible itself—it was okay for some people to be treated like second-class citizens. The Bible plainly says that government has been ordained by God (Romans 13:1). Indeed, leaders of the time pointed to the Bible as validation for their racist laws.

Regardless, the presence and authority of religion in the lives of black Americans has been so strong that it has helped make the modern Black Church the inescapable, omnipresent, all-powerful, infallible institution that it is today. Why is this? Why do African-Americans insist on hanging on to their religion and their god even in the times when they clearly are not serving him and when he clearly is not delivering them?

The African-American version of Christianity tends to be significantly more fear inducing than other brands of Christianity. One can expect the average sermon or church service in a black church to make some reference to hell: why hell is such a scary place, what kinds of people are going to hell, and how to avoid hell. Black children are taught from an early age that dark, scary demons and devils are relentlessly after their very souls and that they must always be sin free lest they die and end up in hell! I remember being a young child and listening to some uncles discuss the existence of "hell hounds"—demonic dogs that can be dispatched by Satan at any time to terrify, torture, and fetch a sinner anywhere in the world. The existence of the hell hounds was, to my uncles, reason enough to "stay prayed up." You cannot imagine the number of terrified, sleepless nights I had, afraid that a hell hound would snatch me out of my bed and drag me to hell if I did not pray without ceasing.

Besides directly teaching about heaven and hell, the Black Church focuses on several other favored topics that are intimately and uniquely tied to one's salvation in a way that is not as obvious in nonblack churches. Sex and sexuality, for example, is one such topic. Because the Black Church rigidly tries to impose many prohibitions on its members and because humans love sex, black leaders have to constantly remind congregants that sex is only for married men and women. Anything outside of that is an abomination that will, without a doubt, lead to eternal burning in the lake of fire.

Submission is another favorite topic. Congregants must submit to their leaders (Hebrews 13:17). Wives must submit to their husbands (Ephesians 5:22–23). Children must submit to their parents (Colossians 3:20). And everyone must submit to Jesus (Ephesians 5:23–24), who is, ironically, submitted to god, who is himself. There is a whole chain of command that must be followed if one does not want to end up in hell. Submission demands obedience and unquestioning loyalty, which creates a breeding ground for abuse of power. "Since urban black community and religiosity are almost incestuously intertwined, faith-based leaders are provided with an especially wide political berth and moral license," writes Hutchinson.[4]

Countless religious adherents around the world and throughout time have been raped, beaten, stolen from, and killed, all while being told they must not complain because they must submit—and so it is in the Black Church. "Church officials should be by very definition above worldly criticism and reproach because of their Christian altruism. In his critique of the unimpeachable status of the religious, Frederick Douglass noted, 'To be an infidel no more proves a man to be selfish, mean and wicked than to be evangelical proves him to be honest, just and humane.'"[5] And since the Bible says that it is the church leaders who pray for the souls of the members, it becomes imperative that the members be in total submission at all times or risk their eternal soul's salvation.

An additional theme found in the Black Church is the concept of demonic possession. Although an obsession with demonic possession certainly exists in other cultures and Christian denominations, its presence in and impact on the Black Church is unique. Any and everything can lead to a person being possessed or affected by demons—whether TV, music, friends, food, activities, thoughts, or jobs. They are all potential doorways for demons to be introduced into a person's life. And how would a woman know if she had a demon in her life? "Signs" include depression, anxiety, sadness, poverty, failed relationships, misfortunes, sickness, death, lost objects, mood swings, lack of faith, failures, disappointments, etc. The list could go on forever. Depending on whom you talk to, if you are not rich, healthy, and happy, you probably have at least one demon affecting your life in some way. So, even though she may be struggling with a host of real-life problems, a black woman must also grapple with the idea that she has demons in her life, which in turn is indicative of the presence of sin in her life. This worry just creates more emotional turmoil.

Other favorite topics include love, faith, gifts and fruit of the spirit, money, and wealth. However, the sad truth is that even the Black Church's seemingly positive and upbeat teachings come attached with a lot of conditions and requirements that are simply unobtainable. The constantly dangling carrot of promises of riches and happiness and salvation causes people to obsessively try to fulfill the requirements, only to fail miserably. And repeated failure is what leads to much heartache and pain.

So, why is there not more conversation in the black community about the role of the church? Why is there not more analysis of the good, the bad, and the ugly? Perhaps some people simply have not made any connections between obvious life problems and the church. Some do not want to think about it while others simply have not thought about it. Some people may be completely apathetic, likely owing to their own nominal belief system. We also know that some people are judgmental from a distance, unable or unwilling to openly criticize the church. "The age-old association of religiosity with morality is particularly ironclad in African American communities. Because religiosity is evidence of 'authentic' blackness, it is difficult for black non-theists to publicly criticize the Black Church's special trifecta of religious dogma, greed, and hubris."[6]

One of the biggest reasons I think that there has not been more conversation about this is that believers are afraid of the "sin" involved in entertaining such thoughts. Cue the Ebony Exodus Project and this book. While I fully support one's right to think and believe whatever one wants, I find it startling that a large number of black people not only do *not* think critically about religion, but they also do not even *want* to think critically about it. There seems to be no desire whatsoever to think critically about something that is so intimately intertwined in their lives, even for nominal Christians.

It has been my experience that white people are much more open to reflecting on these topics, even in general conversation. White people will express their thoughts and entertain others' ideas. Often, these conversations are congenial and transition smoothly to other topics. This typically is not the case for black people. One would think that black people would want to have this type of conversation much more often, especially considering the fact that black women profess and actively exercise their faith in an attempt to build better lives, which, as you will read in this book, are not improving. Black people are comfortable blaming racism and classism. "Rather, the thought of the black churches distinguishes the 'sins' of black people from the 'sin' of white racism, which is considered by far the most wretched. . . . Churches generally give their attention to the fact that all blacks are oppressed by the greater force of white racism, which is considered the greater evil and possibly the sources of all sin."[7] And while the issue of racism certainly has its place in the discourse, it seems only fitting that the institution that claims to have the answers to all of life's ills should likewise be a part of the conversation about how the church itself is contributing to the problems in the black community—not least of which those experienced by black women.

2

BRIA'S STORY

Childhood Experiences
"But when I turned sixteen, my rebellion . . . started."

Bria ("Bree") is a forty-four-year-old black woman who spent her entire childhood and a large portion of her adult life involved in religious activities. Growing up as a Jehovah's Witness introduced her to a world of judgmental insensitivity. In addition to the religiously derived mental and emotional trauma she suffered, she had a negligent mother who was an abusive alcoholic. Although she grew up in what many people thought looked like a healthy home, her story is a classic example of dysfunction brought on largely by the expectations of oppressive religion.

I grew up as a Jehovah's Witness. There wasn't much that we could do except go to the Kingdom Hall and distribute literature. But when I turned sixteen, my rebellion against Jehovah's Witnesses started. And what preceded that was that we couldn't go to a "worldly prom," a prom that wasn't for Jehovah's Witnesses youth. So, a group of us got together and were going to create our own Jehovah's Witnesses prom. I was turning seventeen and I'll never forget. There was a letter we had circulating among the youth about getting together for this prom. The elder read the letter from the platform at the assembly. It was a couple of thousand people under this roof and all these young people are looking at each other like, *How did they get this letter?* So, they pretty much put the kibosh on it right then and there. I got home and I was livid. I looked my father in the eye and I told him, "I don't care what they say. Next year, I will be going to the prom. I will be eighteen. I'm paying for my own stuff. You can threaten me. You can whoop me. You can say whatever you want, but I am going to my prom." And my dad looked at me and he didn't say anything."

Nondenominational Church
"I jumped in with both feet."

Even though Bria left the Jehovah's Witnesses almost immediately after high school, she spent many years continuing to struggle with the guilt and shame that was so deeply engrained in her psyche. After years of vacillation, she found her way into a nondenominational church.

After I graduated high school, I left the Jehovah's Witnesses. I studied different religions, but I had had enough. I was burnt out from going door to door and going to Bible study. After I became a mother, my children went to Sunday school, but it wasn't for me. After I reached my 30s, I started feeling like I needed something. So, on my job this lady evangelized me. I was about thirty or thirty-one years old and she led me to Christ. It was nondenominational, but I couldn't tell because it was charismatic, tongue-talking, laying hands, Pentecostal, and I jumped in with both feet. I was a prophetess. I was an evangelist. I was an intercessory prayer warrior. You name it, I did it. When the church opened, I was there, honey!

But I'm not sure what happened with me. I went from being allowed to participate in the church to being sat down and told I couldn't pray. I was hurt but I submitted and I said, "God, if this is your will, so be it." But the fuckery that I noticed was that the people who had money were treated better. I researched about tithing and when I told them that tithing was in relation to food and not money, I was called Satan. I was called a demon. I was told to not let the devil use me. So, in my private time I said, "God, it's just gonna be me and you." I was very vocal about what was right and what was wrong and I think that's part of what led to me being sat down. They did not like that. The leadership called me Jezebel and said that I was being rebellious.

The very thing that I hated in Christians, that condescending, "Oh, you need Jesus" talk, I hated to hear that. But I noticed I was becoming that. And when I heard myself say, "You need Jesus," it was like somebody slapped the shit out of me. I couldn't believe that I had arrived and found that I was this condescending Christian asshole. I said, "The very thing I hate, now I'm becoming." Eventually I came to a point where I was ashamed to identify myself as Christian.

Relationships and Sex
"'Bitch please!' The thought of being with a man is disgusting!"

Bria says that she's always known that she was a lesbian. Yet, she had heterosexual relationships because she thought it would please god.

I'm not bi. My first sexual experience was with a girl. My parents had no idea. Oh no! Tell a Jehovah's Witness that? No! In the nondenomination church, though, I had homosexual thoughts but not lesbian sex. I said, "God, give me a sign. If I'm not supposed to be gay, give me a sign." So, I went to the church one day and there was this girl on the stage talking about how she was delivered. And I didn't understand what "delivered" meant. I didn't understand that Christian lingo shit. But she was saying she was gay and god had freed her, delivered her, from her homosexual life. I took that as a sign. I got in my car and drove to my gay friend's house and told her that I was going to do this straight and do this thing for Jesus. "Don't try to talk me out of it." And she was like, "OK, cool." I'm a cold turkey kind of person. When I stop smoking, I don't get a goddamn patch. I don't take a pill. I don't chew gum. I stop! And that's what I did. I just stopped. No struggle. And I was fortunate. Because when I first came to the church, if a woman had a big ass, I had to make sure I wasn't like, "Goddamn!"

I didn't look at women but I did fornicate with men. I couldn't just jump into that, though. When the lady that brought me into church said I was going to date men, I almost said, "Bitch please!" But I didn't. I said, "Let me tell you something. I know that you're happy that I'm not gay, but I'm still gay in my head and the thought of being with a man is disgusting!" For about two and a half years, uh-uh! I remember one day I was just driving and I said, "One day me and my husband. . ." And that's when I knew it was in my subconscious. I took that as a sign that, "OK, now I'm ready."

The funny part is that the first time I fornicated was coming from the movie *The Passion of the Christ*. I called one of the ministers and confessed and she said, "Was it worth it?" And I said, "Yes, it was! Yes, it was!" And she just started laughing and said, "Well, just don't do it again." But we did. I just didn't tell her. We felt guilty after that first time but after a while it was just like, "Fuck it! Because we can always repent." That was the good thing about being religious. You get a "Get-Out-of-Jail-Free" card. But he said, "We ought to go ahead and get married." I was like, "You think we should get married just because of sex? Are you kidding me? I'm going to get bored of you and you're going to get bored of me. No!"

Once the newness wore off, I noticed that I wasn't really into marriage. The church really turned me off being married. The church I belonged to was really open. The couples talked about their issues in front of everyone. And I said to myself right there, "Who in the hell would want to get married? This sounds like a curse. Why does the woman have to do all the work? You make excuses for the man. Thanks, but no thanks." When I got saved, I was gay. So, I put that to the side so I could serve god. And every time they mentioned me being married, I threw up. I had a physical reaction to the thought of being married.

So, when it came to submitting, that was something that I laughed at because by that time, I was a control freak. Nothing happened unless Bree had something to say first. The thought of relinquishing that to a man, let alone god! I remember having this conversation with a minister. I said, "How do you give control to something invisible? Something you can't see?" And she said, "Faith. You gotta trust." So, there was a sense of relief when I decided to stop being in control. You know, when you control everything, there's a physical toll on you, and I was definitely feeling that. So, while I did struggle with somebody having this control over my life, there was this sense of relief knowing that I didn't have to be in control of everything. I just had to do what I was told because I was tired.

But then again, when I would hear about these Christian marriage issues, and hear about how if a man was into drugs and if he came home and he had fucked a crack whore and he wanted to sex you up, you had to submit your body. "Bitch! Are you crazy? No! No! No! No! No! You want me to cook for you and you done lied and said you had a hole in your pocket but you done went on a crack binge for three days?" I have a problem with that. You can be a woman. You can be a power broker, or anything, but you just have to submit to that damn man when he gets home? So, I understood submission in theory, but I knew that I would never get married. I can't do it. And even when I did date the guy in church, I ran that. I was in control, and he knew that I told him what to do.

Eventually, I went from being straight for Jesus to being who I am. I didn't need to be reborn. I was born right the first time. I'm a lesbian. I always have been. This is me. And the first people I told were my children. My kids know that I'm open-minded. I'm liberal. In the church, I would always take up for gay people. The Black Church is always dogging out gays. So, that was a sore issue, a sore spot for me.

One Bad Relationship
"I really did hurt him. So, I went back to him and asked for forgiveness."

Bria readily admits that, of all the admonitions of her church, rules about how to be in a relationship with a man did not hold water with her. Bria experienced rejection and was an outcast because of her views on marriage and her unwillingness to go against her conscience. Her childhood history of having to be the responsible one manifested as dysfunction in her adult relationships.

Well, I was bad to him! I was psychologically damaging him! First of all, I was not confident in him as a leader. So, in order to keep him in his place, I used scripture against him because he didn't read the Bible. I learned early about manipulating. It doesn't take long to discover a person's weakness. So, when he would attempt to exert his authority, I would say, "In all your getting, you better get understanding"! (Proverbs 4:7). You know what I'm saying! You better understand who I am. And he would talk about the Proverbs Woman (Proverbs 31) and I would say, "You show me *any* woman who can aspire and who has successfully become that Proverbs Woman and I will sign over every dime I have to her. It's not possible. And you're not about to lord that over my head."

So, my fear prevented me from trusting him and getting to know him as a friend, as a boyfriend. And then, what happened? You get the prophecies. Everybody saying that I'm his wife. He's my husband. We're at church on New Year's and the pastor's hint-hinting to him that I'm his wife. And while that did sound good, I know I am not one of these women whose dream is to get married. Sure, I would like the wedding. I would like the dress, the party, and some presents. But I don't want a marriage. That's not me. And the thought of submitting and trusting another person, that will never happen.

The worse thing was that then we started receiving these invitations. You know the church is cliqued up and it was an insult to me as a human that I was not worthy to fellowship with until I was coupled up and people thought that we were going to get married. "Now y'all wanna let us into the clique?" I told them, "Hell no! Hell no!" And I told him that under no circumstances did I want to deal with them because we weren't good enough before! It's so insulting! Somehow, by being married you're more virtuous. And he didn't understand.

They didn't even give him the time of day until we got together. He wasn't worth crap to them because he didn't dress all that well. But I saw the potential. They even mispronounced his name. That's how much they didn't talk to him. And I would have to correct them. Then he started to look attractive to everybody else. But that's OK because all I knew was that I wanted no part of that. Uh-uh! I didn't want to sit there and gossip. I didn't want to sit there and hear about their damn children. I didn't care who was pregnant. I didn't care. But that was something that he wanted.

He wanted that life but that wasn't for me. And now he's married and he's expecting a child. That's what he wanted.

I just could not respect him. I made it very clear to him that I had no respect for him. But, a couple of years later once I understood and I had a talk with myself, I realized that I really did hurt him. So, I went back to him and asked for forgiveness. And thankfully he forgave me because I did not understand how much I had hurt him until I heard it from him. I just told him, "The thought of anyone being in control of my life, it's just scary. And y'all talking about I gotta submit to you. I gotta fight that." But we are good friends now. He still does that invite-me-to-church shit and I just delete that shit.

Deconversion and the Turning Point
"Question everything."

"Question everything" has become Bria's motto. She now lives her life by the standard of needing to fully understand why she's doing something. It is no longer acceptable to her to just agree with someone or to do something that she doesn't fully understand or accept. Her exodus from religion started through study.

I read the Bible. I started at Genesis and I was sick. I was sick at what I read. First, I stopped praying for people even though they still called me for prayer. I stopped prophesying. I said, "I will not serve a god that is this crazy." See, I had read the Bible before, but I had never dissected it. I would just read it like a story. When I read how he hardened Pharaoh's heart was, I didn't use critical thinking skills. Why would he harden Pharaoh's heart (Exodus 4:21, 7:3, and 14:4)? Why would you make a bet with Satan over Job (Job 1:6–12 and 2:1–7)? See, previously when I read the story, I never paid attention to any of that. Why is it that when Job questioned god, he's *getting smart?* You know, being a smart ass with him? So, all these questions started swirling around and I noticed that I could not rationalize it. Nor would I excuse this behavior.

I then became agnostic because agnostic was still better than saying "I'm an atheist." But I could not use that word "agnostic" because it did not fit. I did not believe in god. I totally rejected god. I was an atheist in my heart, but I was not willing to admit it to anyone.

The church doesn't really foster critical thinking. Not at all. What's so funny is that I had a religion class and that is what did it. My teacher, an awesome Howard-educated black man who was also a minister, showed me that there was an Egyptian god, Horus, who was also just like Jesus who was worshiped before Jesus. That was it! When he told me that, it was a wrap. It was a fucking wrap. I was done. He does not know that it was him and his keeping-it-real ass that had me say, "DEUCES!" to religion. Oh! That was it, when I studied that for myself! And then I Googled "gods born of a virgin," and all of this shit came up! I said, "Christianity is a quilt and they took pieces from other beliefs, sewed that shit together, and called it Christianity." I was done!

A lot of people go by Pascal's Wager, "What if?" OK, you can take out Jesus and put any god there. What if? What if you've done all of this and you find out that it's Allah. You're fucked in this game just like I am. Or Horus? Or Zeus? You're just like I am. You're fucked, too! Pascal just happened to be Christian. When you put another god there, then they look stupid. And I'm not going to let that gamble make me believe in any god.

I told my children, question everything. Question everything. Question why you go to church. Question why you read the Bible. When I said that I was an atheist out loud, I was scared. I thought the sky was literally going to open up. What if, after I say I'm an atheist, he proves that he's a god? Well, I'm still here.

Coming Out: Lost Friendships and Relationships
"I didn't know that I was still fucking affected by Jehovah's Witnesses twenty-five years later."

If you can't tell by the story so far, Bria is one tough cookie. She has strong opinions and an even stronger courage of conviction. While some might call her tone harsh, her story demonstrates how hard she had to fight to reclaim her peace of mind after years of religion's abuses. During the interview, she exposed just how deep the hurt and pain was that was perpetuated by religion. During this part of the conversation, she began to cry.

Officially, I've been out for about three years, but I've been an atheist for about five. I just took to the Internet to look for a community where I could be an atheist and it was OK. But when I decided to let everyone know that I was an atheist, I changed my religious belief on Facebook. That's how I told everybody I was an atheist. I said, "Fuck it!" I had stopped going to church, but I had some church members as friends. When I changed that status to atheist, ooohhhhh. . . Oh my god! I didn't understand the power of the Internet until I changed it, because I went from being a Christian to being spiritual to being don't-say-nothing-to-me-about-god to being just like, "Fuck it! I'm an atheist." And man! I got questioned. People started coming on my wall. Then I got de-friended.

My mother cussed me out. Oh yes! My mother was disfellowshipped from Jehovah's Witnesses in the 1980s. But it's funny how when I came out as an atheist, then she believes in god. She said, "God help you! God help you!" I told her, "Why don't you ask him to help you with your drinking? And then you can ask him to help me. You want to turn this on and off but let's prioritize. You got a drinking problem. I don't." So, me and my mother, our relationship, I terminated it this past winter. It wasn't hard because, like I said, I've been in charge of the house and the family since I was a kid. So, I don't have a relationship with my mother or my brother. I was born into that family but there's no connection there. My friends and my children are my family. My sister and I have no relationship. I have a relationship with one aunt, her children, and my dad. I'm sure he knows I'm an atheist, but I didn't tell him I'm an atheist because I don't like disappointing my father. I was expecting my dad to abide by the Jehovah's Witnesses bylaws and not have anything to do with me, but he has continued conversation with me. I was glad to have that. So, I do not talk to him about church and he does not talk to me about Kingdom Hall. He doesn't care; I just didn't have the heart to tell my dad.

But my grandmother? She would have nothing to do with me. I have not talked to my grandmother, I'll be forty-three. . . . Oh, I'm about to cry. I have not talked to my grandmother since I was eighteen when I had graduated school. When I came to visit in California, my grandmother was outside and I said, "Ooo, I'm gonna go out there and speak to my granny." And my sister said, "Uh-uh. Don't go out there because she doesn't want to see you." WHOA! You know. My mother was very physically abusive and my grandmother was instrumental in helping me stay sane. So, to know that our relationship was over like that, over religion! Really? So, I have some resentment. My grandmother is about ninety-five. If she died, I wouldn't go to the funeral. I wouldn't even go because I have resentment. I will be there for my father. But I'm still angry. I would probably spit on her grave because I just feel that your love for your child should be stronger than you love for the Watch Tower Bible and Tract Society. Until this talk, this is the first time that I ever acknowledged that. I didn't know that I was still fucking affected by Jehovah's Witnesses twenty-five years later.

There were many people who stopped being my friend. Some of them really hurt. I know they went and gossiped about it. I almost cried, but then I was like, "Fuck them bitches!" So, I put on my Facebook, "Educate yourself! Before you go gossiping at church, educate yourself." But then I started getting friend requests from people at church who I knew didn't even like me. So, why are you trying to be nosey? Ignore! *You barely talked to me when I was at church, so why are you sending me a friend request?*

The lady that led me to Christ, she kept inviting me to this religious stuff and I was like, "Fuck it! I am an atheist!" I hated to tell her that because she is real holy-holy, but it wasn't going to stop if I didn't say it. But, you know what she told me? "So, you think that because you don't love god I'm going to stop loving you?" When she told me that, I went to church with her! I said, "You know what? If this women who is sold out! Sanctified! Can say that? The least I can do is support her. The least I can do is go to her church. It's two hours out of my life. It ain't gonna kill me." They would rather you say you're a crackhead, junky, motherfucking cannibal, lesbian than say you are an atheist. And she said to me, "You are still my daughter. I love you. My BFF." I told her I was an atheist, and she's gangster like me and she just said, "So! So what? You still my sister?"

So, I do have Christians who are in my inner circle and I tell them to be themselves. If you pray for your food, pray for your food. You don't have to change because I'm here. I'm not going to burst in flames. If you want to say, "Thank you Jesus," say it. I'm not funny like that. But, if I don't HALLELUJAH with you, just don't trip because, if you sneeze, I'm not going to say, "Bless you." I'll say, "Girl, you'll be alright."

After I came out, I created Black Freethinkers on Facebook. And that grew to about 350–400 people, then I took if off Facebook and brought it to a main site. So, we got on Tumblr because there are so many people who are like, *I'm atheist. I'm black. Now what?* For some people, if you're a freethinker, it doesn't mean you're an atheist. It could mean that you're agnostic or you go to church and you're questioning. So, you can come to our group and there's absolutely no drama.

Problems with the Church
"It takes no intelligence to be a Christian. But, if you are a freethinker, honey, you better know your stuff!"

After years of experience in different types of Christian sects and denominations, Bria has a unique perspective on what she believes to be the major problems with religion and especially the Black Church.

The church is a straight up hustle. Me and my atheist friend, we say we are going to open up a church. We need some money. We are going to open up us a church. It's the biggest grind out there. And it takes no intelligence to be a Christian. But, if you are a freethinker, honey, you better know your stuff! I'm not mad at these pastors for working the church out their money. What I am mad at is that you can find out that your pastor is fucking a fourteen-year-old but you don't want to believe it. *The devil's tempting. God's testing.* You don't want to read your Bible to find out if what I'm saying to you is actually true. Willful ignorance! That's the biggest problem. They say, "Tithe and watch you get back a thousand fold." How do you even know what a thousand fold is? How do you measure that? I was a poor tither. Hell! That might be why they sat me down. I was a poor tither. I may have tithed four times out of the years that I was at church. But I still went from having nothing to having a nice apartment and a good job despite the fact that I didn't tithe.

It ain't god. We cut up whether we are saved or not. We're more scared of the people and what they think. We're scared of being rejected by our own community. That's why we have all these gays and sissies in the church that can't come out freely. Why? Because they know the church is going to be gossiping. You might be starving and your kids don't have anything to eat, but you're scared to tell anybody because, as soon as you tell one person, next thing you know you're going to hear about your shit being preached about from the pulpit. That's what happened to me. I told somebody something in confidence and, next thing I knew, my shit was on the platform being talked about. And how is that for your self-esteem? But people came back every week for some more. And why? "Because god called me to this church." Why? Because they're scared.

This is a black community thing. How do they control us? Fear! Fear! You're scared not to go to church. You feel guilty if you decide, *Oh, I don't feel like going to church this weekend. I'mma sleep in.* Now you feel guilty because somebody is going to call you and ask why you didn't go to church. "You missed a good service. Somebody asked about you." You're going to deal with some guilt. Especially women. To me, a woman wasn't taken seriously unless she was a mother of the church or unless she was wailing and prevailing and presenting at a shut-in. Unless she was important to the church, she wasn't worth the time of day.

When it felt right to leave that church, I vowed to never become the member of another church. And I didn't. I did go to different churches and, at this one church I went to, there was a woman pastor. She was cuckoo for Coco Puffs. She was very rude, but she respected me because I was a "prophetess." I went to her church twice. When I sat in her church and watched her berate adults that had their own children, when I sat and listened to this woman talk because they didn't tithe or because they didn't do an offering or she didn't think they were being cheerful givers, I told the woman that led me to Christ, "I can't come back. I cannot watch this." The pastor was known for calling you "Saints" and "Ain'ts." "Saints, please come up and leave your offering. Ain'ts, you can rise." If her husband would minister, he would say, "Who doesn't know what god has for their life? Stand up. I'mma pray for you." And this is what really happened: she stood up and took those people out one by one. "What you mean you don't know what god has for your life? Didn't me and you pray about this? Didn't god give you a word and tell you to do this? Didn't. . ." POW! "Now sit down! Didn't me and you talk about this?" POW! "Sit down!" It was like being at the carnival and shooting those ducks as they pass by! "Girl!" I said, "I will never come here again."

But you tell me. Why should he answer your prayers? What makes you more important than all these babies in the world? They didn't ask to come here. All they want is sustenance. But they won't see that today because they're going to die and become food for vultures and got flies hanging around because they are dying on the inside. And tell my why is it that your prayer to get a husband or a job is more important than feeding these babies. And if your god is that fucked up to answer your prayer and not these boney-ass mothers with these hellafied stomachs sticking out and their teeth sticking out because they have become a skeleton, if he is that sick to answer your prayer instead of them, fuck your Jesus. Fuck him.

When I really want to be a smart ass, I will say, "How fucking weak is your god if you can't even hold a conversation with somebody who's a Wiccan? You can't even talk to a Satanist." But, *what a mighty god we serve? What an awesome god? God is an awesome god.* You can't sit and engage and learn why a Satanist is a Satanist. You will trip out if you go to the fucking cash register and your fucking total comes out to $6.66. Your license plate can't say 666. So, help me understand. How fucked up is your god if this kind of shit fucks you up? That's not saying too much for your god.

Psychological and Emotional Toll
"You aspire to be perfect and pleasing unto the lord and it's just not possible."

According to how she believes the Black Church judges people, Bria has multiple strikes against her. First, she is a woman and women tend to be

undervalued in churches. Second, she's a lesbian. She also had two children
out of wedlock. In all of her struggles and turmoil, she has had very few people
in her life provide her with consistent and loving support. As a result, Bria
has suffered many painful events in her life that left her depressed and alone.

I think the biggest affect that it had on me psychologically and emotionally
was guilt. When I left the Jehovah's Witnesses at eighteen, that was all
I knew. All I knew were the people, the adults and children that I grew
up with. I got baptized at seventeen at Dodger Stadium. My friends and
I were in line waiting and I knew I had no business getting baptized. I
knew it! But the pioneer that I studied with told me that I was ready.
And, what the hell? She was a pioneer. Wouldn't she know more than
me? So, I got baptized at seventeen. And at eighteen, I was gone. I didn't
cuss. I just said "F this." At eighteen I left and I got pregnant at nineteen.
I felt that Jehovah was mad. I felt too guilty to pray for a healthy baby
because Jehovah was mad. I had guilt.

I had my daughter in Michigan, but I had this postpartum depression
I was struggling with and I went back to California. You go back to what
you're familiar with. I went back to the Kingdom Hall on a Tuesday
night. I think my daughter was about five months. The elders called me
in the back and I thought, *What the hell they want with me?* This was my
first time back in two years. I was dating my first love, the guy I lost my
virginity to. He wasn't baptized. So, they told me to stop seeing him.
And I said "NO!" And they told me that he wasn't an approved associate.
And I said "So what? He's a Jehovah's Witness. He's been raised in the
Kingdom Hall ever since we were kids." They said, "So, are you going
to stop seeing him?" "No, I am not," I said, and I got my daughter and
I left. And the next thing I know, they disfellowshipped me. Oh yeah.
They disfellowshipped my black ass. And even though I knew that I had
no intention of being a Jehovah's Witness ever again, there was this shock
that resonated because I know that if I ever see these people again, I'm
going to be invisible because I'm disfellowshipped. That means that all
the children that I grew up with, all the people that we went out to
dinner with, would now consider me dead.

Even though I had tears in my eyes when my dad called me, I put this brave front on and said, "Daddy, that's the best news you could have ever told me." I had to put on this brave front. I was shocked. I was absolutely shocked because I knew there was no turning back now. It was a new kind of sadness.

I remember when my aunt died. I am not close to my family now and I wasn't close before I became an atheist. I was born into this family, but we just have nothing in common.

The one ally I had, my aunt, went into the hospital when I was about thirty or thirty-one. I went into her room and I knew she was dead. She was a fucking corpse. Officially she was alive but technically she was dead. I knew that woman was dead. I didn't need a doctor to tell me that. So, after they confirmed that she was dying, they took her off the machine and she died. She stopped breathing and my other aunt said, "Jesus loves you, Bree. Jesus loves you."

Now, all that hatred, all those curse words I wanted to say, I had kept them inside of me out of respect for my aunt, the one that died. But goddammit, my aunt was dead. So, I wasn't breaking any promises. Girl, I went hard on their asses. "Bitch!" I said, "Fuck you and your Jesus, Bitch! You wasn't thinking about Jesus when you talked about me. You talked about my children. And now you want to get holy holy. And now you want to tell me that you love me and so does Jesus." And I said, "If I could kill all of y'all motherfuckers, I would." See, my perception of a Christian was "Hypocrite."

But, I became depressed like many people in the church, especially women, because you aspire to be perfect and pleasing unto the lord. And it's just not possible. It's just not possible. You are depressed. You're calling yourself worthless. You're not worthy. *I'm a wretch.* (Fuck you, Jesus! I am somebody and so are my children.) At some point I was so depressed that I thought it would be best if I just died. If I could have just found a nonpainful way to do it, I would have. Jesus said the only unforgivable sin was blasphemy. So, I was rationalizing. *That means I can commit suicide because the only unforgivable sin was blasphemy. So, I can kill myself and still go to heaven.* Because I was just fucking depressed. I can tell you this, though. I have not been depressed since I left, since I acknowledged that I don't know if god exists.

I would know if god exists if he would cure every terminal illness or feed all these starving babies fucking dying. I was on Facebook and this Christian girl was so upset with me because there was a picture in which I had tagged myself and it said, "19,000 children will die of starvation today. Why should god answer your prayer?" I asked her, "Why you upset? All you gotta do is answer the question." Why should he answer your prayer when he got bigger fish to fry?

Physical Health
"You better stop claiming that nonsense!"

Bria attests to one of the more insidious problems within the Black Church—distrust of medical professionals and a dependence on prayer, fasting, and positive confession to address illness.

It was big time at my nondenominational church to use prayer and confession for health. It was an insult. It almost got ugly.

"I'm sick."

"Why you claiming that?"

"Bitch! Because I'm sick! I ain't claiming shit! I'm sick!"

OR

"I got allergies."

"No you don't. Stop claiming that."

OR

"I got cancer,"

"OK, let's go get some blessing oil. We gonna pray for Sister Bree. She's dealing with some serious health issues now. We gonna anoint her."

How come you can believe that? How can you believe that I got cancer, but you can't believe that I got some damn allergies? I would rather have some damn allergies than cancer!

The sad part is that we bring it home. "Mama, I don't feel good." "Stop claiming that, man." I remember my son had this fever. Now, this stuff has been indoctrinated in me. My son was burning up with this fever—I think he might have been about thirteen—and I didn't take him to the hospital. You know what I did? I woke him up and said, "Son, if you gotta confess anything, confess it and this fever will go away. Ask god to forgive you." Never mind that my son could use a dose of Tylenol to break that fever. "Son, confess your sins. I ain't judging you. Don't worry. You ain't gone get in any trouble. Just confess it. Confess your sins and ask god to forgive you." See, now I had brought this shit home. I remember that clear as day. And what was he going to do? He was going to trust mom and do what she tells him to do.

The pastor did talk about the importance of exercising. He did talk about the importance of medicine because he has sarcoidosis, a lung disease. But, god didn't heal him from that to this day. He still has that to this day.

I do remember this woman—gosh, she was an amazing woman. She was a black woman who, like many of us, didn't do the breast exam. She went for a physical and immediately after feeling her breast, she was in the hospital. They told her, "Put on this gown. We are admitting you immediately." So, word gets back. She was stage four. She went from thinking she just had a regular damn-ass doctor's appointment to having stage four cancer. I remember them praying, "We not gonna receive that word from the doctor." I swear I remember her saying she was cured. And I remember telling my brother, because my brother got prostate cancer, "You ain't gotta receive that cause there's this woman in my church, she got stage four cancer and she got healed." And my brother looked at me like I was crazy. But I really believed she was healed. Girl, a year and a half later, she was dead and I was confused. I was like, "Hold up!" Because I remember them saying she was healed. So, how could she be dead? And you know what the pastor said, "She got her final healing." What! That's what he said. *She got her final healing.*

Effect on Kids
"When you got all these people telling you who you're supposed to be and who you should be with, that's a recipe for disaster."

Richard Dawkins is fond of warning that people should avoid labeling their child with religious terms. It is a growing concern in the nonreligious community that children are indoctrinated with harmful and sometimes abusive belief systems starting from early childhood. The children who are forced to be at church all day every day with their parents and who appear to be the best children in the church often end up being the ones with the most problems, despite the fact that these children were likely seen as "golden children" in the church and received favoritism. Bria highlights how putting that sort of pressure on young children arrests normal development and leads to problems later in life.

I think the part that hurt me most was that the children that were shined upon were the ones that ended up getting pregnant, were the ones who ended up smoking and drinking, were the ones who almost caught a case of statutory rape. Expectations! When the church as a whole has these expectations for you and your life, that's a recipe for disaster. When you have all these people telling you who you're supposed to be and who you should be with, that's a recipe for disaster.

We had this one sweet girl who everybody at the church knew was fast as hell. We knew this girl was hot! So, when she came before the church and said she had dedicated her body to god, it took everything in my might to not go, "Girl, bye!" She ended up getting pregnant in high school. And I was mad at the church with the favoritism and the nepotism. This favoritism was a lot to witness because I've always been for the underdog.

Hope for the Future
"There's about to be some changes…"

Despite the hell that Bria has been through in her life, she now leads a happy and full life free from religious oppression. Although she sees a lot of problems within the black community, problems she believes often stem from black churches, she is still hopeful for the ever-increasing number of black men and women who are choosing to make the exodus from religion. Her final thoughts are ones of hope.

The fight has been there for black people; the fight has been there for women; the fight has been there for gays, lesbians, bisexual, transgendered. Now, there's about to be some changes coming down for atheists and skeptics.

3

CRYSTAL'S STORY

Childhood Experiences
"If you just go a half a millimeter further then you will see that Jesus cannot be real."

Crystal is a twenty-four-year-old woman living abroad. Her religious upbringing consisted of attending different types of churches with her parents. She tells a story of having a mother who believed in god but was freethinking enough to try to protect her children against sexism and hypocrisy.

I grew up in the church mostly. The church we went to was *nondenominational*. My mom mostly grew up in church. My dad became more of a religious person once he met my mom and they got married. When I was a baby, they were in church together under the House of God. But my memories are mainly of when they were at separate denominations. My dad became a Seventh-day Adventist when I was in elementary school, maybe five or six years old. My mom still went to her church. My dad still went to his church.

I remember one time my mom asked my dad to come with us. I thought, *I don't think my daddy really wants to go*. But he came anyway and once we got to my mom's church, I just felt he really wasn't comfortable. On another occasion, my mom actually visited my dad's Seventh-day Adventist Church and there I could feel that she didn't really feel comfortable there either. But my parents divorced when I was about ten. So, I got different views and experiences of being in different types of churches. That's been most of my religious upbringing. I had exposure to church, sometimes two or three times a week. It was definitely a bulk of my childhood experience.

As far as my growing up in the Seventh-day Adventist Church, my dad went to church every Saturday and we went with him. It was a very calm environment. Sometimes he would actually fall asleep in church. My dad would always stay up late until 2 a.m. in the morning, because he is an artist. Maybe that's why he was tired. It's definitely more of a calmer environment and the pastor wasn't out there barking at people and bossing them or bullying them around.

I've always loved to read. We would go on Saturday in the morning to school and after that we would go upstairs to the sanctuary, and church would begin. As a nine- or ten-year-old kid, I would be bored in the sermon. So my dad would let me bring my books to church, and I would be sitting in the pew reading *The Baby-sitters Club* and nobody said anything.

My mother was very faithful, but the issue she had trouble with was the position of men and women in the church. As far as being the head, men are allowed to do things like raise their voices at women. There was a sexist issue she spoke out about and the pastor asked her to leave because she spoke up. She saw something that she didn't agree with and, with her having three sons, it was something that she did not want around them—the way she saw women being treated in the church. So, when I was thirteen, she was asked to leave the church and, after a few months, he gave her "permission" to come back to the church. Then, a year later, when I was fourteen, another issue came up that my mother spoke out about and, again, she was asked to leave. That gave me something to think about. *How can you ask someone to leave a church because they may have done something that you didn't approve of or they may have spoken up about something?*

So, for me, that set a positive example. My mom saw something she didn't agree with and she spoke up and I was so proud of that. I wasn't there when it happened, but she did talk about the issue and I really thought she was right. There are things you shouldn't have to put up with. You do have a choice to say no. You have a choice to say, "*I don't want to be a part of this.*"

She still was faithful and it didn't change her viewpoint on god. She still found other churches to visit. And being still under her roof as a teenager, if she wanted to visit a certain church, she would take us with her. She still didn't lose her faith, but I guess maybe my mom wanted a break. Maybe she wanted to clear her head about a few things. So, between the ages of fifteen, sixteen, seventeen, we weren't really a part of any regular church. I was still spending weekends with my dad and he got remarried when I was thirteen. We would still go to the Seventh-day Adventist Church with him and my stepmom.

I remember. I was thirteen. It was 1999 and Destiny's Child's *Writings on the Wall* CD had come out, and my dad had just gotten married to my stepmom. I was spending the weekend with them and I was playing the Destiny's Child CD with my stepsister, and my stepmom said, "Oh, I don't want you to play that music!" She didn't agree with "secular music." So, I respected them. But my mom wasn't really like that because my mom was into all kinds of music. She loves all kinds of music but she's never said, "Secular music this! God's music that!" My dad, too. He's got all kinds of music. Also, in my early teens, I was reading a lot of those black romance types of books and I would bring them over. She would say, "I don't want you to bring these kinds of books in." I thought, *OK, goodness gracious*!

Growing up, my parents did not celebrate Christmas and they did not celebrate Easter. So, we never had Easter and Christmas because my parents had researched the whole pagan reason behind Easter and Christmas. How this is borrowed! Where Easter comes from! How it is rooted in paganism. So, it just had me question. If they researched this, did they purposely push other things in their minds away? Because, if you have all this and you know where it comes from, if you just go a half a millimeter further then you will see that Jesus cannot be real. It just makes me wonder.

Early Twenties
"I wasn't really going on a regular basis. I just didn't have time for it."

In college, Crystal participated only minimally in religious activities, even though she still held on to her beliefs.

When I got to college I was already on my own. I wasn't part of a regular church. My campus did have a few Bible study groups that I went to a couple of times, and our campus sponsored a couple of revivals that one of the student religious organizations held. But for the most part, by then I wasn't really going on a regular basis. I just didn't have time for it. Around eighteen, nineteen, twenty we were just here and there, but I still had beliefs in God and still prayed and read my Bible here and there.

Problems for the Kids
"The father came in with a belt and he said, "You need to talk Crystal, you need to talk."

Although Crystal's parents were supportive of her freethinking tendencies, Crystal was not able to escape many of the evils that affect young children in church, such as corporal punishment and lies about evolution. Today Crystal reflects on how disturbing some of her experiences were.

As an adult now, I can think more critically about a lot of the meanness and things I saw like corporal punishment, the way kids were being whipped in church by the elders. I guess my memory faded a little as far as minute details, but there was always a general message: *You don't do this. You don't do that.* Or, *keep your kids under control.* It was just really a fear-based kind of thing, and as a kid, there was always this fear: *I hope I don't get a whipping.*

They never whipped me and my brothers, but I was always thinking, *I hope I don't do something that is going to make them mad at me.* There was a lot of fear-based preaching, especially with the whole heaven and hell messages and the casting out of demons or spirits.

When I was eleven, we asked our church members, "What about dinosaurs?" They said dinosaurs don't exist, and I thought, *What about all the bones in the ground? Did god put those there too?* I don't have all the answers. I don't know how this world got here, but we live in a huge galaxy with all these planets. There are some things that I can't answer, but I'm not going to say there is a god just because that's the generally accepted belief. I'm not just going to believe because that's what most people are told they should believe in. All of the creation questions that religion attempts to answer, I don't believe. It just doesn't make sense to me. It just doesn't.

For me as a child, I was more of an introvert. I have my extrovert moments, but overall, I've always been quiet, the listener who just takes everything in. It's just part of my personality. There were times when we would have youth conventions or youth summits for a week in the summer and they would have something for the kids to talk about. They would take us on outings and have rap sessions for us to talk about our issues. For some reason, they would always make me feel bad for being quiet. *"You need to talk more."*

I remember when I was seven and I spent a certain amount of time with this family who was part of our church. I traveled with them for the summer. They had eight or nine kids. I was hanging out with them and they had a church convention in North Carolina. There was one particular time the mom was doing my hair and I was with her and her daughters and she said "Chris, so, you need to talk more. You need to talk more. Why aren't you talking? Why aren't you talking?" And the father came in with a belt and he said, "You need to talk, Crystal. You need to talk." I said, "Why?" and I was really crying. "What's wrong? What am I doing wrong?" There is nothing wrong with me! I'm just a quiet type of child. I thought, *why are you threatening me with a belt? Let me just be who I am. Let me just be myself.* It really scared me as a kid. That never really left my memory.

Sex and Relationships

"I know for me, when I do get married, I would prefer that the man that I'm with share the same views of nonbelief."

Religion impacted Crystal's early ideas about sex and relationships in some of the typical ways. Not only did it impact dating, but it also affected her ability to maintain friendships. Interestingly enough, in college Crystal found herself drifting from a boyfriend because of his family's religious beliefs, which were more conservative than her own. Even though she is no longer a believer, Crystal is still a virgin and maintains her personal beliefs about what role sex should play in romantic relationships. She reflects on how religion often prevents people from being free to develop their own moral code for themselves.

As early as eleven, I remember that they preached about fornication. *You shouldn't have sex before marriage.* They would have these little sessions with the preteens and the teenagers on why we shouldn't have sex before marriage. They would sometimes separate the girls from the guys and sometimes they would have us all talking together. They never talked about condoms or anything like that. It was just that you should never have sex.

There was one girl in particular who we knew was having sex, and they were always getting on her. Her father was in the church and he was a widower. She was his only daughter and they were always on her. They would take her behind closed doors and have these little meetings with her. I knew what they were talking about because we were close and she would tell me. She would invite me over to hang out and to sleep over. I know my mom did not want me to hang around with her that much. She was seventeen years old and having sex and everybody knew this. They were trying to help her "get on the right track."

In high school we weren't really in church regularly, but at that time I still wanted to save myself for marriage. I still believed in the fornication message and that sex was for marriage. I didn't really date too many guys or have a serious boyfriend. There was one guy in particular that I had this thing for and we would meet up with each other. He didn't go to my school, but I knew where he lived. He would kiss me and we would have our little make-out sessions. And then I would say, "I have to go to school," and that was it. Throughout high school I didn't really have any serious romantic relationships. I still thought, *"I don't want to have sex until I'm married."*

In my sophomore year in college, I started dating a guy that was very religious. His father was actually the pastor of his church. With him being a pastor's kid, that relationship moved fast. I knew that with this guy there would not be anything jumping off unless we decided that we were going to be together forever. His father was religious and this guy thought, *Oh my God, I think she's the one! Oh, I really love you.* But we had only been together a few weeks. Then, he took me to his church to meet his dad who said, "My son is very important to me. I don't want you to break his heart." I thought, *We've only been together two weeks. Calm down.*

I would go to church with him because I was trying to make a good impression for his father and everybody in church. It was one of those small churches. The membership was fifteen or twenty. Everybody got really emotionally invested and it just felt like it was happening too fast. So, we were together for a few months, but we ended up just breaking off because we just became more distant. That was the end of my junior year, and I would say that was the last serious relationship I was in. That was maybe four or five years ago. I've been single since then. But even in college those early years, I still thought sex is for marriage.

Since I became a nonbeliever, I really find myself asking, "Why is that such a big message in the church?" I know people say that the Bible says no fornication, but that's a book written by a man. Why is it so important? Looking at society in general, what's the big deal? Why is there so much emotional investment in not having sex before marriage? For me now, what matters is whether or not you're a mature adult and you are educated about sex. If you are educated about condoms and other ways to prevent pregnancies and you are emotionally ready and your partner is emotionally ready to handle it, then it's OK. The message preached to me when I was younger was, *You shouldn't do it because you are going to go to hell.* How do you know anyway? What makes you come to that conclusion? Just because it's in the Bible?

I think it is such a double standard. It's OK if the guy is out there doing his thing. It's not so much pressure. There's more pressure on the women to not have premarital sex. In society across the board, it is not as big a deal if the guy isn't a virgin as opposed to the woman. Her virginity is her most important thing. There is more to my personality than whether I'm a virgin or not. I think we create these ideas, these ideologies, about how it should be. Since I became a nonbeliever, I've opened my mind to so much more. What gives you the right to tell someone how they should live their sex life?

Another problem is that gay people are bashed. I think gay people should have a right to get married. My aunt is gay. When my mom told me she was gay, she said it like it was the worst thing. I said, "OK. So I still love her, she's family. It doesn't make her a bad person." I support people if they are gay and they want to get married. How can you discriminate or hate somebody just because they don't follow the heterosexual orientation? Is that the only legitimate way for people to live? Religion just helps perpetuate these privileges and dominant ideas.

Financial Impact
"The whole pressure that's placed on offering, now as an adult, I can think more critically about it."

Crystal witnessed two extremes regarding tithing and offering in the church.

I know these churches operate as businesses. They have to find a way to operate. So, they collect two or three offerings, sometimes even bullying people by saying, "We don't have enough money. We need you to give another offering." What's up with that? In the Seventh-day Adventist Church, I noticed that they had a different vibe. They collected one offering. They passed a collection plate and that was it.

Coming Out
"I have to be honest. . . . It is hard sometimes."

Like many nonbelievers, Crystal's deconversion started with research. Her interest in the history of Christianity and her discovering how much of the religion is derived from previous religions had a profound impact on her ability to maintain her faith. And while she's found that there are some areas in her life in which her lack of belief has not been a problem, it has caused issues in other areas. Because of this, at the time of the interview, she was still trying to find a way to manage the effects of nonbelief on a black woman's life.

I haven't told many people that I'm a nonbeliever. I actually told my dad the first time last summer. We were at a restaurant and the strangest thing happened. We prayed for our meal and then I thought, *This is my dad and we're very close so let me just tell him.* And the shocking thing was he told me, "Well actually, Chris, I no longer believe either. The reason I asked you if you wanted to pray is because I thought you still believed." I said, "Actually I don't. I was praying just because of you." He didn't say "atheist," but he said, "There are things that I just no longer believe in. I still have my doubts. Maybe I believe in god. Maybe there is a god. Maybe there isn't."

For me, it started with the Internet. These days we've got YouTube and, with all this technology, it is so much easier. So, my brother told me about this documentary called *Zeitgeist*. I won't take everything as fact but when I watched it on YouTube, I thought, *That was interesting, let me investigate it some more.* The first part dealt with religion. They talked about the origins of Christianity and how much has been borrowed.

Even though I put religion on one hand and the belief in god on the other, I still believe that, in some ways, they intersect. After watching *Zeitgeist,* I went out and did some research. This information had been presented to me and I thought, *Let me not accept it all without doing my own reading.* I just started going to my campus library. I found this book called *Forgery in Christianity.* I also found an e-book *Pagan & Christian Creeds: Their Origin and Meaning.* It's all been created.

I started asking all of these questions in my mind. *How can we prove that there is a heaven and hell? And why do they come to that conclusion that when we die we are going to end up in one or the other? How do you know what to begin with?* And I started doubting if there is a god. *Is it necessary to believe there is one?* All these other societies had different beliefs of a god. To me, religion and belief in god always implies that there's a right or wrong and a type of finality. *How do you know that's the final end? How do you know that god is it?* This implies an absolute finality. I don't believe there is absolute truth.

I've shared with my mom things that I don't believe in anymore. I was sharing with her the information about the pagan origins of Christianity, and she just had this scared look in her face. She said, "Sometimes we may need religion." And I just said, "Well, this doesn't make sense to me anymore." Actually, it surprised me that I felt so free. Growing up with, "You're going to do this or you are going to hell if you don't believe in that." Maybe that experience impacted the feeling I felt when I stopped believing. And I just felt free. I haven't really outright said I'm an atheist. I don't want to be confined to a label. Because I don't accept society's agreed-upon definition of what God is, I understand that that makes me an atheist. However, I don't want to feel as if that is all there is to my identity.

I stopped believing in 2010. I came out on Facebook. I posted on my profile an article I found called "Black Women and the A-word." I haven't told many people about my nonbelief, but I thought it would give people something to think about and maybe they would start to ask me. Another black girl that I met here where I'm living commented on it. She's a strong believer and it's been pretty hard. I hung out with her and a few other black girls living here. She invited me to a gospel concert organized by the local chapter of her sorority. I didn't know it was a gospel concert until I got there. But when I got there and I saw the pulpit and I thought, *Oh my God! This is a gospel concert.* I felt just like I was back in church. But since I grew up in church, I could still pretend. I knew what to expect.

Later that night we had dinner with a few other people who came to the concert and they asked me, "Do you have any religion?" I said that I didn't have any religion and that I didn't believe. It was hard for me to say. So, one of the girls next to me asked me to tell her why I don't believe. I wanted to keep it brief because it was dinner. I didn't want to make it the general table conversation, so I just told her briefly that there are some things I've researched and I don't really believe there is a Jesus. I also said that I don't feel that makes me a bad person, but there are just some things that I no longer believe in. She really had this sad look on her face. The girl who invited me, I think she overheard and her demeanor changed for the rest of the evening. I thought, *I'm just expressing my views. I have not once attacked anybody for believing what they believe. I still respect your belief, please respect my nonbelief.* I actually felt that the whole harmony for the evening changed. But I had to be honest. I have to be honest with myself and I have to be more comfortable with telling people that I don't believe. But it is hard sometimes.

Problems with the Church
"If I am anywhere and somebody is attacking somebody, I would say, 'This is not the kind of place I need to be.'"

While Crystal reflects on many problems with the Black Church, her story makes it clear that she is most concerned about sexism in the church.

I noticed one thing about the church that I spent the bulk of my childhood in. Our pastor was very opinionated and, at the time, there were things he would say that, as a little kid, I would be scared about. I would think, *That's a pretty mean thing to say.*

There were just all kinds of issues my mom had and I noticed in my church sexism and the way women were treated. There were several other women in the church who were married. Like my mom's situation, their husbands did not come to church with them. There were those rare occasions when the husband would come, maybe just to make the wife happy or maybe the pastor was getting on them. "Your husband, he's not in church, why not?" My church they did the whole laying of the hands, you know, pass people out, put a sheet over them.

One particular time this one woman's husband was there. The pastor was just attacking him. "Why are you not in church?" The pastor just clawed him out and then it became a situation where everybody was on the pastor's side against this one husband. He had probably only been to this church a couple of times. It's just the attacking and that sort of thing that makes me wonder how it may have made my mom feel. Maybe that's why she pushed my dad to come to church with her a few times. It was not a really positive atmosphere and environment.

It was a small church, for the most part, our membership maybe stayed around fifty or sixty. Our churches have normally been those storefront types. We would have visitors to the church and literally, if the pastor didn't like someone's spirit or attitude, he would say, "Get out of my church right now!" He would literally kick people out. So it was that kind of fear-based, bringing people down environment. *Do this. Do that.* Or, *I don't like what you are saying. I don't like your vibe. Get out of my church.*

If I am anywhere and somebody is attacking somebody else, I would say, "This is not the kind of place I need to be at." I just couldn't be in that kind of environment. I know that many people are in those kinds of church environments, and I just wonder what makes certain pastors have this fear-based kind of preaching and what makes the people stay?

There was definitely this vibe that "we're the right religion." I think religion perpetuates a lot of issues because of the lack of acceptance of people and of other cultures. Growing up in church, we were told that you should only be a Christian. The Muslims got it wrong. Or those Jehovah Witnesses got it wrong. It's just all this disharmony. We happen to grow up in the United States. We happen to have our ancestors brought over here, and this is our circumstance. We could have been born Korean, and a large percentage of people in that society, about 50/50, have no religion, no belief, or no affiliation and the other half are either Buddhist or Christians. Do you think that if I had been born somewhere else, I would be going to hell?

We all go through the same emotions and we have all these religions. The whole right and wrong and how we are pointing fingers just creates more division. Even with the terrorism issue, we are invading countries in the Middle East because they think differently. I believe in basic human rights. I don't believe that people should be tortured or denied certain rights as human beings. Religion creates animosity and intolerance.

Moving Forward
"If you had to give up your belief in god, what would that start with?"

Crystal says that leaving religion has made her a more compassionate person, accepting of all religious systems. She sees life as a journey and encourages others—believers and nonbelievers alike—to see life as more than a person's religious label.

We definitely have a ton of information, and I think it has really helped. There wasn't Facebook or YouTube ten or fifteen years ago. There is such a wealth in knowledge now and I wonder if that scares certain religious organizations. They might say, "Oh my God! There is all this information out here. We still have to make sure that we keep these people in line with their beliefs." When I put that article up about black women and atheism, one girl had put on my wall, "You know there was a time when I was questioning my beliefs." Why is it wrong to question your beliefs? If you are questioning it, then ask yourself why. Research and get answers to those questions.

Everyone is entitled to think and feel as they choose. However, as much as I embraced the freedom of declaring my departure from religious and theistic ideas, I found myself becoming tolerant of our differences as humans beings. There is no universal truth, just our subjective and relative opinions about how we view reality and existence. Everyone has a certain "truth" that they believe in and that's fine. It makes the world colorful. If you had to give up your belief in God, what would that start with? As humans, we have this need for duality or dualism. We need to have the good versus evil, black versus white, God versus Satan and heaven versus hell.

What I don't like, and this applies to believers and nonbelievers, is when we begin to feel our way is the only way and those on the other side are wrong. While I'm not religious or a theist in the traditional sense, I still believe in the power of our minds to mold and shape our actions which has an impact on creating the reality we see and feel around us. If we focus on the negative, negativity will come our way. Focus on the positive and you'll be awake to the possibilities that exist around you and take the action necessary to mold the reality and future you see for yourself. I'm more in tune to what I feel and what my intuition reveals to me. My intuition never ceases to surprise me and I've started to call it my inner god. So, that's where I am. I don't want to be stuck in a label and I'm open to the changes my mind will go through as I get further in this journey called life.

The Best Part
"Even now, I don't fear."

Crystal reflects on the value of her mother's advice, which, despite their different views on religion, serves her well.

You should not live in fear. Even though my mom is still in church, one thing I do appreciate her telling me was, "Don't ever do something or follow something out of fear, because if you react out of fear you are doing it for the wrong reasons." Even now, I don't fear. If people say there is a God, I don't accept that and I don't fear that I don't accept it. I'm not afraid of that.

4

ON MENTAL
AND EMOTIONAL HEALTH

"My Soul Refused to be Comforted. I remembered God and was troubled."
—*Psalms 77:2–3*

One basic explanation for depression is that it is anger turned inward. In black communities, black women have a lot to be angry about. They are under constant strain to be the backbones of their families, to care for the men and children, and to work and provide financially. Also, black woman have to deal with the unfortunate reality that black men are painfully absent from the home. Black men die disproportionately more from murder and HIV/AIDS than any other group of American men.[1] Additionally, black men are disproportionately incarcerated, undereducated, and unemployed. So, black women face much of the day-to-day pressures of caring for their families alone. They have cause to be angry. The realities of life in black communities also contribute to mental illness. Chronic stress can lead to decreased levels of the mood-related brain chemicals serotonin, dopamine, and norepinephrine. And a lack of them leads to depression.

Fuss. Fight. Yell.
The Angry Black Woman

Although the research is scant, there is cause to believe that black women suffer mental and emotional problems disproportionately more than other racial and ethnic females. Therefore, they are likely to fall victim to many stereotypes that stem from those types of problems. One such negative stereotype is that of the Angry Black Woman. As we know, stereotypes usually stem from gross overgeneralizations of things that may have some basis in reality. So, where does the Angry Black Woman stereotype come from? Well, we see her on TV, in movies, and on talk shows all the time. She is always fussing at her husband, boyfriend, children, coworkers, or anyone else unfortunate enough to find themselves in her presence. Take, for example, a car commercial that was out a few years ago. In it a crowd of people scramble through a dealership to try to claim the car they want before someone else gets to it. The white woman gets in front of hers and, with a smile, politely tells an approaching man that she has claimed it already. A white man does the same thing, except with a little more excitement in his eyes. What does the black woman do? She rolls her eyes, rolls her neck, and, with a little flick of her wrist and pointing of her finger, says, "Uh-uh! This one is mine!" You can see this vividly in your mind based on just this brief description because many of us have known people who do, in reality, behave this way. But more significantly, we have seen the caricature repeated over and over in the media. The idea that black women are perpetually angry is in our collective consciousness.

An Angry Black Woman can also be found at the head of many black families. Since African-American families tend to be extremely matriarchal, older black women find themselves in the uniquely overburdened position of caring for, guiding, and preserving large extended families plagued by multiple broken homes, undereducation, poverty, chronic illness, drug addiction, and legal problems. These women have likely been leaders in their families since they were teenagers, and they have spent their entire lives in service to others. We praise and revere our matriarchs in the black community, because we recognize that they have survived decades of pain, heart break, and setbacks by being strong. And sometimes being strong means learning to suppress emotions and taking a no-nonsense approach to childrearing. In the end, although we know our matriarchs love us, it is not unusual to hear black people comment about how mean grandma is or how, "She don't play!"

> Black women are told that they are tough, pushy, and in charge rather than soft, feminine, and vulnerable. The image makes her someone to be feared rather than someone to be loved. These stereotypes render Black women as caricatures instead of whole people with strengths and weaknesses, tender sides and tough edges.... However, because the myth of unshakability has also become so embedded in the collective psyche of the Black community, African American women often find that they are not allowed to be vulnerable or needy, even among their own.[2]

The Black Church has a role to play in creating this dynamic in the black community. In addition to all of the demands placed on black women, those who are greatly involved in church are faced with never-ending expectations not only from their families, but also from their churches. Since it is visibly obvious that black women compose a larger portion of the church than black men, it is no wonder that they are the ones who handle the cleaning, bookkeeping, shopping, and day-to-day business of the church. They also make up the choirs, pastors' committees, and usher boards. Since the average church has fewer than one hundred members,[3] and they are usually struggling day to day just to keep the doors open, these hardworking women work for free and with little recognition. But the men who lead the church get doted on daily.

Submit. Serve. Smile.
The Highly Committed Woman

Depression and exhaustion are often the real culprits behind what appears to be anger. "If you're trying to identify depression in Black women, one of the first things to look for is a woman who is working very hard and seems disconnected from her own needs." [4] Is it any wonder then that the woman who has to smile and submit and serve for every Sunday and Wednesday service, Thursday and Saturday choir rehearsal, Friday prayer meeting, and Monday committee meeting goes home at the end of the day with little positive energy to give her family? Says Hutchinson, "Constructions of mainstream African-American female gender roles and social responsibilities are unquestionably linked to religious observance."[5] As Charisse C. Jones and Kumea Shorter-Gooden note,

> Wonderfully talented, hard-working, selfless women often shift and suppress their own needs for so long that they are pushed insidiously, unwittingly, often invisibly, toward depression. They suffer from what we call the Sisterella complex, a manifestation of depression that is all too common in Black American women today. Much like the classic Cinderella character, Sisterella is the Black women who honors others but denies herself. She achieves in her own right—indeed, she may overachieve—yet she works tirelessly, sometimes masochistically, to promote, protect, and appease others. She is trying so hard to be what others want and need that she has lost control of the shifting process. It's overtaken her. Sisterella has had to give too much to others. Or she's given up too much of herself. She has so internalized society's messages that say she is less capable, less valuable, that she has stopped trying to prove otherwise. She has lost sight of her own gifts as well as her own needs. Her identity is confused, her personal goals are deeply buried, and she shrinks inwardly. She becomes depressed, sometimes severely so.[6]

One way that black churches contribute to the development of depression in black women is by the insistence that depression is not real or that it is somehow the fault of the sufferer. The black community is notorious for its unwillingness to seek medical care. There are many reasons why this is true, and some reasons are well-founded, such as a deep-seated distrust of the predominantly white medical establishment because of past abuses. But regardless of the reason, the result is the same—chronic illness that goes untreated. Black churches teach that people need to primarily depend on god, the Bible, faith, and prayer to get their needs met. Worse still is the fact that black churches often adamantly discourage seeking professional mental, emotional, or psychological help because, after all, depression and other mental illnesses are not real. Tell an average black pastor that you are feeling down and you will probably be advised to attend church, read the Bible, or pray more.

Unfortunately, when the teachings and philosophies of black churches are combined with fear and distrust of the medical community, black women face a unique internal conflict in their attempts to identify and treat their depression symptoms. Black families tend to believe that mental illness is a sign of weakness and that a person taking psychotropic medication must be crazy. Black women pride themselves on being strong in the face of adversity. If they admit that they are depressed, they are also admitting that they are weak. Weakness. Shame. Sin. Guilt. Doubt. Fault. Demons. These are just a few of the scary words that are closely intertwined with depression and other mental illnesses in the minds of black churches. Sadly for the black woman, this spells a lifetime of suffering.

A paragraph on Mental Health America's Web page about depression in black women accurately reflects the typical sentiments of black women toward depression:

> The myths and stigma that surround depression create needless pain and confusion, and can keep people from getting proper treatment. The following statements reflect some common misconceptions about African Americans and depression: "*Why are you depressed? If our people could make it through slavery, we can make it through anything.*" "*When a black woman suffers from a mental disorder, the opinion is that she is weak. And weakness in black women is intolerable.*" "*You should take your troubles to Jesus, not some stranger/psychiatrist.*" The truth is that getting help is a sign of strength. People with depression can't just "snap out of it."[7]

Try. Sin. Fail.
The Minimally Committed Woman

Even the woman who is not overly involved in church but who was raised in church or attends occasionally will not be able to fully escape emotional and psychological damage. In fact, it is the minimally involved black woman who might suffer the most, because she is usually eaten from the inside out with guilt, regret, and worry. If she is not completely "sold out" to Jesus, she probably worries about her unrepentant sin. For example, she may be having sex with her boyfriend or going to the club on Saturday night, but on Sunday morning, she will be told that her sinful life will put her in hell. If she has children, she is constantly being told that she should "train up a child in the way that he should go" (Proverbs 22:6) so that she can guarantee the safety, health, and success of her children. If she does not dedicate her children back to the lord, she might lose them at any time. After all, as the thinking goes, children belong to the lord and they are only on loan to us. If we will not raise them properly, god has every right to take them from us at any time. Can you imagine the psychological damage that hearing that kind of message would play on a young mother's mind? It is worse than being investigated by Child Protective Services because at least there are set laws as to what constitutes abuse and neglect. In the church, those laws seem to change weekly, and they are based on one pastor's interpretation of any given verse. Some research suggests that the moderately religious person may actually experience more depression than the extremely devout or the completely nonreligious.[8]

No matter how good a mother, productive a citizen, smart a student, or diligent a worker, a black woman who is minimally committed to church will be faced with ridicule and will likely be outcast by many other women in the church. "Images of black women faithfully shuttling their children to church and socializing them into Christianaity are prominent in mainstream black culture. If being black and being Christian are synonymous, then being black, female, and religious or 'spiritual' (whatever the denomination or belief system) is practically compulsory."[9] Most minimally committed black women change churches multiple times in their lives because they always end up feeling out of place in a church. No matter how friendly or accepting the church may appear on the surface, the messages of sin, hell, death, and fear will be an integral part of doctrine in almost every black church they encounter. For many, there is no alternative to this churchgoing path. As Sikivu Hutchinson rightly points out, "even on a casual level, religiosity is never far from day-to-day African American life."[10]

Paralysis

God is love.
- *"Beloved, let us love one another: for love is of God." (1 John 4:7)*
- *"And we have known and believed the love that god hath to us. God is love." (1 John 4:16)*

Love is patient and kind and is not jealous.
- *"Love is patient. Love is kind. It does not envy." (1 Corinthians 13:4 NIV)*

God is jealous, wrathful, and vengeful. This sentiment is revealed in numerous biblical verses. To name just a handful:
- *"For I am jealous over you." (2 Corinthians 11:2)*
- *"Thou shalt not bow down thyself to them, nor serve them: for I the LORD thy God am a jealous God." (Exodus 20:5)*
- *"For thou shalt worship no other god: for the LORD, whose name is Jealous, is a jealous God." (Exodus 34:14)*
- *"For the LORD thy God is a jealous God." (Deuteronomy 6:15)*
- *"God is jealous, and the LORD revengeth." (Nahum 1:2)*
- *"Let no man deceive you with vain words: for because of these things cometh the wrath of God upon the children of disobedience." (Ephesians 5:6)*
- *And I will execute great vengeance upon them with furious rebukes; and they shall know that I [am] the LORD, when I shall lay my vengeance upon them." (Ezekiel 25:17)*

Since being jealous, wrathful, and vengeful and being loving seem to be incompatible, either god is not love or he is not jealous. And since the Bible reiterates over one hundred times how jealous, wrathful, and vengeful god is—while only talking about his love a few dozen times— one could reason that he would much prefer to be known as a jealous, wrathful, and vengeful god than as a god of love and patience.

The church could not operate in its present form without fear. The hierarchy, commandments, rules, and laws are all directed at forcing people to do what someone else has determined to be best. Of course, the benefactors are the ones who have power and control and want to keep it that way. Wherever there is fear, there is emotional and psychological damage. For black women, being indoctrinated in traditional black-church thinking can cause several kinds of fear-based paralysis.

The first kind of paralysis is the result of waiting on prayers to be answered. This creates a need for signs and confirmation. An otherwise intelligent and confident woman may become paralyzed with fear because she does not want to make a mistake that might cause god to become angry with her. Women in this state are looking everywhere for proof that they are on the right track. They will not turn right or left with just any kind of undefined evidence. But the problem is that what constitutes proof or evidence is constantly changing. Sometimes it presents itself as a random Bible scripture. Sometimes it is a sermon by the pastor or a televangelist. Sometimes it is a song on the radio, a kind word from a stranger, or bumping into a friend in public. These black women become paralyzed because they will not make a move without some sort of confirmation, despite the fact that there are no rules about what confirmation will look like when it presents itself. Black women in this state strongly identify with women in the Bible such as Ruth (Book of Ruth), who did not make decisions for herself but instead depended on the guidance of her most trusted family member, Naomi. These women also refer to biblical examples of mistakes. A good example is the story of when Sarah made the rash decision to offer her maid to her husband, Abraham, to have a child (Genesis 16:2–6). This story serves as proof of the consequences of making important decisions without waiting on god's guidance. The interesting thing is that once this type of woman gets what she believes to be confirmation, she will go forward boldly with the "calling" or direction given. But this kind of zeal almost always leads to the second kind of paralysis.

The second kind of paralysis is the result of experiencing years of the first kind of paralysis and being disappointed as a result. When a woman has spent years doing everything the "right" way, only to still experience a lot of failure, she becomes paralyzed with a different kind of fear. While the previous form of paralysis results from trying to avoid making mistakes, this paralysis comes from the belief that she has already made so many mistakes that she needs to be even more vigilant about preventing mistakes. She begins to regretfully identify herself with the short-sighted and guilt-ridden version of Sarah, because she feels she has made a lot of mistakes. Remember, she previously waited on signs and confirmation before making any decision, and once she received that confirmation, she would pursue god's directives with passion and excited commitment. Given the nature of life, however, she would invariably experience disappointment and failure. Of course, in her mind, god could not have led her wrong. If she was disappointed or had failed in some way, it must have been her own fault. As a result, she blames herself for being too impatient, for not waiting on the lord, or for being proud. This constant cycle of waiting on signs, proceeding once getting a sign, seeing failure, then blaming herself for making poor decisions causes this woman to become frozen. She is now unable to make a choice for herself. She is constantly afraid that she has some kind of sin in her life or is not dedicated to church and god enough and, in her mind, those are the reasons for so much heartache in her life.

One can already predict the overall consequences of such a mind-set. Once a woman is experiencing this kind of paralysis, she will stay with an abusive husband, neglect her children, forgo college, or refuse a job promotion because it might interfere with the tasks she needs to complete in order to please god. Because of the level of spiritual angst and frustration the women in this state are experiencing, depression is inevitable. Sadly, these women believe that the only possible explanations for such repeated failure, disappointment, and heartache are that the woman is missing the mark somewhere or that god and his Bible are liars. And "god is not a man that he should lie." (Numbers 23:19)

Too Blessed to Be Stressed

It is very common to hear black church folk say things like, "I'm too blessed to be stressed" or "I'm too blessed to be depressed." The phrases are often heard in the context of conversations about a lot of stress. Black women turn to these rapt clichés when they need to "confess" something positive. Confession in the Black Church is exactly opposite of confession in the Catholic Church. To Catholics, confession means talking about and admitting to the sin that is in one's life, that is, sin that has actually occurred, even if the sin is in the mind or heart. In the Black Church, confession is about declaring as true something desirable that has not happened yet. So, if I want a new job, I "confess" on a regular basis that I have a new job. The people to whom I am making the confession understand that I am not lying. This concept was born from an interpretation of the creation stories in Genesis in which god spoke into existence all things of creation. Add that to the various scriptures that say we are like god and, VOILÀ! You've got a new spin on an old practice—confession in reverse.

So, when Black women are declaring, "I'm too blessed to be depressed," what they are actually saying is, "I'm very stressed or depressed and I'm tired of feeling this way." Sadly, the latter sentence is unacceptable in the Black Church. Prosperity and healing ministers like T. D. Jakes, Creflo Dollar, Benny Hinn, and others teach that the creative power of god is in every human being's tongue. Whatever you speak is what will manifest. If you admit that you are stressed or depressed, you will only experience more stress and depression.

The negative implications are clear. As with so many other situations, black women find themselves in the position of not being able to get real help for real problems in the number one place they would expect to get that help—church. Instead of being able to honestly say that they are stressed, depressed, overwhelmed, and burnt out, they have to say that they are happy and peaceful and fulfilled. They have to declare, as true, the things they want to experience, not the things they are actually experiencing. One might think that surely these women will have someone to whom they can tell the full truth. Unfortunately, that is not always the case. For the "sold out" or devout black Christian, she may find herself utterly alone, even with her friends. If she spends all of her time only with other devout Christians and tries to tell the truth, she will find herself getting lots of feedback reminding her to make a positive confession. When she tries to talk to people for support, she will probably end up feeling guilty about having said such terrible things. She will be afraid that she has just created more negativity in her life.

While the power of positive thinking is well known and generally accepted as having some beneficial effects on emotional health, this type of positivity is more than that. Modern concepts of positive thinking acknowledge what is wrong while also setting goals and dreams for the future. Positive thinking is also about focusing on positive things that are already in one's life while still exploring ways to improve life. Positive confession, on the other hand, is just the opposite. It is about ignoring or blatantly denying the existence of negative or undesirable things in one's life. On her Web site, televangelist Joyce Meyer posts a list of daily confessions. One such confession blatantly states, "I don't speak negative things."[11] Point blank. In talking about her own struggles with depression, she also says:

> For many years of my life, I experienced regular depression. I would awaken many mornings with a little voice in my head saying, "I feel depressed." I believed this was my own thought, not realizing that it was Satan making suggestions to me through my mind. Later, when God drew me into a closer walk with Him and I began seriously studying His Word, I learned that I didn't have to follow every feeling and thought that I had. I began to speak aloud and say, "I will not be depressed." I learned to put on the garment of praise spoken of in Isaiah 61:3. We may not always feel like praising, but a victorious person does not have the luxury of living by feelings.[12]

This sort of thinking is born of an overdependence on supernatural intervention. Prayer. Begging. Expecting. Waiting on god to do something instead of making it happen for yourself.

Depression as the Result of Sin

Besides an absence of a positive confession, there are other believed sources of depression. If a black woman is displaying symptoms of depression, it may be the result of her own sin. She may be doing something wrong or simply lacking faith. If the problem truly is that she lacks faith or is in sin, the thinking is that the depression will not go away with medication or psychotherapy. Healing only comes through faith. If the woman does not have enough faith, it is usually because she does not pray, read her Bible, or attend church enough.

The problem could also be other things she is doing. It could be because she watches scary movies or because she is sleeping with a man to whom she is not married. Maybe she does not submit to her husband the way she should. Or perhaps she has not been paying her tithes faithfully. The list of possible sins is endless and it depends on what her church and pastor teach. Some preachers, T. D. Jakes, for example, take a seemingly empathetic approach to a woman's struggles with depression. In a sermon titled "Dealing with Depression," Jakes takes this unassuming stance of compassion, which he succinctly ends with a tiny phrase that plants the seed that the woman's problems are in some way of her own making.

> I know what it is to have a good time but can't hold it. Can't keep it. I know what it is to have fleeting feelings of happiness and contentment and then sink into the despair of my predicament. I know what is it to ache in my soul where aspirins don't go and need something and not know what it is and need it so long that I give up that I'm ever going to get it and then give up and let the currents of despair wash away my personality and I drown in a situation that I could have walked on. That's the miracle of Jesus walking on the water. That's why he rebuked Peter for having little faith cause when Peter started sinking he said, "Man you're sinking in something you could have been walking on." I just wonder. Are you sinking in something that you could've been walking on?[13]

It is simply a nicer, more poetic way of saying, "You are not doing something right. Get it together." Even when they say things like, "I understand that the world has hurt you," they often couple it with phrases like, "You have to pray your way out of it" or "You need to pray for more faith." Sometimes when faith healers make an alter call for issues like depression—which they often do—people coming forward for prayer is considered to be a sign that the minister is a prophet. However, it is simply another indication that depression runs rampant in churches. Everyone knows that black women are under a lot of stress and pressure. Therefore, there is a really strong possibility that, if the pastor makes a call by saying something like, "There's someone in this audience who's been very depressed," someone will respond. It is not a supernatural gift; it is an admission that depression is real and everyone knows it.

Demonic Possession

The worse explanation for depression is that a depressed woman is possessed or has a demon "attached" to her. Not all black churches buy into the concept of "deliverance" (the process of casting out a demon, much like exorcism), but most believe that the devil and demons are real and that they can negatively affect our lives. They may believe that the black woman who is experiencing depression probably has demons in her life and that they have become attached to her because of some sin she has committed. To the church member who believes this way, the only way to get rid of the depression is to get rid of the demon.

Mark 5 tells the story of the man with demons named Legion. In this story, the man is described as living in tombs. The people had tried to bind him with chains many times, but he would always break out of them. So, he spent his time in the tombs, screaming and cutting himself day and night, the story says. When Jesus came along, he cast the demons out of the man and allowed them to possess a heard of swine. Afterward, the townspeople find the man "sitting, clothed, and in his right mind" (Mark 5:15). It took an exorcism for this man to be sane again.

Clearly, placing so much blame on the sufferer does not help with her recovery. The sense of guilt and shame that comes from being told that one has a demon and needs to stop sinning only feeds into the self-hatred, anxiety, and hopelessness that goes with depression. What is worse is that the dialogue between the woman and her pastor about her depression, faith, sin, and demons often occurs in a public forum in front of the entire church. When the woman joins the alter call for prayer, some ministers will use her story as a teachable moment for other members who might be going through some of the same things. So, the shame intensifies. The depression deepens and the cycle continues.

Religion is a detriment to healthy psychological and emotional development. When you add the conservative religious expectations of the Black Church to existing risk factors for mental health problems, the results are predictable. In other words, black women are going to struggle the most in the area of mental health because the socioeconomic stressors of their day-to-day lives are magnified many times over by their religious beliefs. As the women's stories in this book show, religion, especially in the form of the Black Church, has a lot to answer for when considering the mental health of black women. The two cannot be separated.

5

JANET'S STORY

Childhood Experiences
"It was common knowledge that God existed—
so, I believed the same thing."

Janet is a twenty-three-year old woman who was raised primarily by her grandmother. Like many older black women who care for grandchildren, her grandmother raised her in the church. But rather than feeling that church was boring and pointless, as many young children feel, Janet enjoyed going to church. Janet describes her younger self as a "good girl" and part of being a good girl meant having real faith in god. And she really believed.

My grandma taught me the same thing they were taught. I would go to church with her all the time. If she didn't go, I would always find a way to go to church. I was pretty devoted. Like most black people from the South, she was a very religious Christian. She used to talk about God constantly, which all the Black people did. It was never really forced on me. I was just told that it was right, and I grew up to believe that because I was a good kid. It wasn't only her. It was just a common thing. It was common knowledge that God existed—so, I believed the same thing, that's what I was told.

When I moved out here to California and I started living with my mother, I tried to find my own place in church and I pretty much

79

followed everything as much as I could. I was always active and devoted. Since my mother did not go to church, people's parents would give me a ride to church.

Deconversion
"It didn't take a lot of time."

A lifelong and avid reader, teenage Janet didn't have a hard time analyzing the Bible and coming to the conclusion that it couldn't be true.

I think I was bored at one time and I didn't have anything to do. I had nothing to do in the summer when I was little. I was by myself a lot and I used to teach myself stuff because I couldn't go anywhere. I tried to read passages in the Bible when I was younger. But as a high school freshman, I decided to read the Bible, and I was going to take notes. I wanted to get more knowledge. I thought, *Well, let me go through the Bible and I'm going to make notes and start figuring out everything about it.* I mean, every line, everything was important to me.

I started reading about how the Bible was translated and I was wondering what the original language was. So, I started reading all that and then I started taking into account the dinosaurs and how weird that was that dinosaurs weren't mentioned. I was two pages in and pretty much thinking, *This is bullshit!* Then I decided to read about old religions and mainstream religions. I then started thinking about the fact that I am black. I started thinking that since black people were originally African and we were brought from Africa to the United States, then this religion was forced upon the slaves. In Africa, they had their own beliefs and tribes. Everywhere was different. Taking all that into account, I realized that god did not exist.

It was quite a few months that I had been doing this, but it didn't take a lot of time. In the ninth grade, I became agnostic first and I starting joining a lot of agnostic and atheist groups online. I eventually came around to becoming an atheist. That probably took a little bit longer for me to do. There were a lot of difficulties for me to take on that label because I was so strong in my Christian beliefs prior. I mean, everyone around me believes and it would have been harder for me to say that I didn't believe completely. But by saying, *I don't know*, it just makes life simpler. If no one knows, then there could be a god. I didn't want to take that leap to say, *No there isn't*. Actually, it was just a matter of me not being strong enough to assert my opinion. I didn't want to be a major outcast.

Later on in life, though, when I told my grandmother that I didn't believe, she said she loved me no matter what. She didn't make a heavy argument. She kind of took my word for it because I was a big kid and she knows that I'm smart.

Terrible Things Happen
"I was really angry that something happened to me and God would basically hate me for that."

Janet strived hard to be a faithful Christian, but when she was sexually assaulted, she felt guilty because she was no longer a virgin. Not only did she have to deal with the psychological and emotional trauma of the event itself, but she also had to fight through a second layer of religious spiritual angst.

Well, I guess in a way it bothered me for a moment. I had been sexually assaulted and in the Bible it says that you can't do certain things. When I experienced my second sexual trauma, this time with penetration, I became upset because I was such a good person and I was following everything. So as far as my virginity went, the situation was weird. I wasn't going to do the sex-before-marriage thing. That just made me distraught because I felt that I had done something wrong, even though in reality it wasn't me being wrong. I had said no repeatedly when it happened. I felt that I was going to go to hell because something happened to me that I really didn't want to happen to me.

I think that was the biggest emotional thing that bothered me. I was really angry that something happened to me and God would basically hate me for that. Then when I was reading scripture regarding stoning women and stuff like that, I thought that was just completely wrong. I felt it was wrong! It didn't really align with what I believed about how society should work.

The Devil Is Not Imaginary
"I mean I hated the color red."

Like a lot of young black children, Janet had to overcome a fear that was created by insidious stories of the devil and hell.

The devil. . . my whole portrait from my grandma was that he was red. She scared me. I didn't like taking a bath when I was younger. She told me that if I stayed in there too long this devil guy will come out and get me. I was always terrified of the devil. I mean I hated the color red. I had nightmares about the devil getting me. But now, I haven't had one since I was a kid and now red is my favorite color.

Money
"I think it got funnier as I got older."

As a child, Janet tried to be compliant with rules about giving. But, as she grew up and became more knowledgeable about Christianity, her opinions about giving changed.

Yes, we used to always put money in the envelope and put our names on it. They're always big on that. So, whenever I could, I'd give money. I thought I was doing something good and god would reward me for giving the money. I think it got funnier as I got older. I mean, you're really just giving money to the pastor. At the church that I went to, my friend was a pastor and he stopped working because he didn't want to work on Sunday and I always felt it was stupid to give him money because I knew him and he wasn't working. He could have just gotten a job. That was around the time when I started questioning things, so I stopped giving.

Problems with Culture and the Church
"A lot of ideas were forced on us."

Janet does not want to blame all of the problems within the black community on the church, but she believes that the church contributes to existing problems.

I don't know about the Black Church. I feel that, in general, black people just don't think about anything. We don't question anything. We don't try to recognize that a lot of ideas were forced on us. I am very serious about the way that my culture has put certain things in our heads. Our whole society is based on *not* thinking. I don't know why. I can't say I blame the church, but I think it helps contribute.

6

TANIA'S STORY

Childhood Experiences
"Growing up, I just became very frustrated."

Tania is a thirty-eight-year-old woman who calls herself Journey because of her experiences, challenges, and transformations. Growing up in a strict apostolic family, the adolescent Tania struggled to maintain a balance between her religious identity and her personality.

I was brought up in the church. I was raised by my grandmother, but even when I had visitation with my mother, my mother would always make sure we went to church. My grandmother was apostolic. What that means is that I went to church all the time. There were things that I could not participate in because I couldn't wear pants. I couldn't participate in things like PE or other typical things that, as a teenager, you're used to being able to do with your friends. I could not go the movies or attend any social events. So, growing up, I just became very frustrated. Even the thought of me talking with a boy, I may be arousing him in some sense. So, I had to abstain from that.

I guess while my father was incarcerated he had become a minister. So, when he was released, I went to live with him and it was a continuance of all the same religious background. It was just really hard on me. I remember one time I had tried out for the cheerleading team and there were some issues with that because the skirts were so short. And having to go to the pastor and get approval, it was just really hard because it was something that I really wanted to do. Even though I did get that approval, initially I was so embarrassed because the pastor could have just said that he didn't feel like it was appropriate. But I had made the cheerleading team and they also had tryouts for the palm squad. Then that became an issues again because not only am I cheering but now I'm dancing. So, I had a little bit more of an issue there with the palm squad because it was dancing. I thought, *Man! How is god going to be angry that I'm out there dancing or cheering for a team? It's not like I'm intentionally trying to entice the men.* I just always enjoyed dancing and the art of it.

Double Standards and Sexuality
"I always knew in my spirit that I was up there basically singing a lie."

Tania witnessed a lot of hypocrisy growing up and she struggled to reconcile her sexual identity with what she felt in her heart, especially because of the "sin" she saw in the church, her family, and herself.

When I lived with my grandma, she was dating the deacon. The deacon was married. That was a big family secret for so many years. Then, I had an aunt who was dating a well-known pastor in California and he would go to the state she lived in to visit her. So, I just remember looking at that situation and looking at them and thinking, *Wow! Are they serious? You have such total control over my life by using religion. You guys are up here preaching something in front of the congregation but yet I'm seeing something different.* It was a double standard. It was just very, very difficult for me to deal with that.

As I got older, I was on the usher board and sang in the choir. I tried to stay involved in the church because I enjoyed the singing. I enjoyed the fellowship with my friends. But at the same time, I also had a lot of conviction about it. I must have been about twenty years old. I was dealing with this man who was about eight or ten years older than me who was going through a supposed divorce. They had been separated for something like six years. But he would say, "Oh, we can't really be open. We gotta keep this on the low because I'm still technically married." But I felt there was no real point because we were not married. I felt that to shack with anybody or live with anybody, whether it is sexual or not, was not okay and I was going to feel convicted. So, I'm like, "Okay. When are we gonna get married?" And he kept giving me this long, drawn-out excuse that he was still in love with his wife and he was just trying to wait to see if she was going to come back to him. I guess that, in his heart, he felt that god was going to reconcile them. But, yes, in the meantime he wanted to come over and have me cook and do all the things that a wife would do. But yet at the same time, he was not willing to make that commitment to me.

I've always been attracted to women. I've known since a really young age. Maybe eight years old. Maybe younger. That's not something that I decided one day I wanted to be. It's just that ever since I was a child, I always saw women as being very beautiful. Very artistic in some kind of way. It was just something about them and I always knew in my spirit that I was up there basically singing a lie. Even when I tried to have a relationship with a guy, it was out of a biblical conviction. I wanted god to know that I loved him. I was just telling god how sorry I was that maybe I had disappointed him in some sense with my lifestyle. I said, "If it is meant for you to take this thing away from me, this desire, this attraction for women, I would ask you to do that." But at the same time, I was conflicted. I was torn. This is something that I knew was in me.

I'll tell you that, over the last couple of years, I just began to go back and think of some things. My whole issue is that people would get into debates with me about homosexuality and try to get me to shake the demons and maybe go and get some exorcism. With homosexuality, a lot of people feel like it's just about the lusting aspect of the relationship. They don't realize that some of the same issues that I deal with with women, I used to deal with with guys. It's no different. It's all about human relationships.

One thing I just couldn't understand was that I felt like there were more people in the garden than just Adam and Eve. If not, there had to be some incest that was going on because she continued to procreate to populate the earth. If she's just giving birth to her own, her own would've had to have slept together in order for the world to continue. So, why would this god be so judgmental toward me to say that I'm going to go to hell for sleeping with a woman, but yet he procreated the earth with a woman whose children all had to sleep with one other in order to keep the world going. Some Christians have said to me that, yes, in the beginning god did allow incest, but after they were kicked out of the garden he made it an abomination. I was like, "What! So you mean a god would create the world in that way then turn around and curse the people." I was just so blown away.

In today's world, men are always supposed to be the head. I think that's why Adam comes first. It's part of the control thing. They're supposed to be in control and over you and women are to be, more or less, seen and not necessarily heard. And for a long time, women didn't have a voice in the church and if you spoke out they thought you were Eve. You were the fall of man and so you need to get somewhere and sit down and shut up. I think it was a form of control, the fact that they wanted men to be first.

Fear
"I would just do whatever the church said . . . in order to feel like I was going to heaven."

Tania recognizes that fear played an undue role in her life, both as a child and as a young adult. She attests to not only the overt ways in which fear is implanted into churchgoers' minds but also to the implied meanings behind certain doctrines and expectations.

Like I said, here lately I've just being doing a lot of soul searching, just looking back over my life at different things where fear has played a part in my religion. Initially, when I was religious, I feared everything. If I saw people who even looked like they just weren't Christian, a god-fearing person, I allowed fear to overcome me. I feared going to church and I feared not going. Because if I didn't go it was like, "Oh, you didn't go to church last Sunday and you know god don't like that. You can't be stepping away from the house of the lord." I may have gone to church everyday all week but, because I missed one day, there was this fear that god was looking at that and now I'm going to hell. I'll be spending all of my days in hell, just fire and brimstone and gnashing of teeth. All of that. I would just do whatever the church said, whatever the church was doing. I had to do that in order to feel like I was going to heaven.

During service after the minister has finished speaking, of course there's always this alter call. So, the alter call was very intriguing for me as a child because I wanted to see somebody get up there. They were going to be shaking and crying and passing out. The sisters of the church were going to be fanning them. As a child, it was more like a show. I just wanted to go to church to see who was going to shout. You know. "Brother so-and-so, he be getting down!" So, I didn't really put so much into it until once I became a teenager and into my adult years. That's when the fear really set in. The church expects that you now have an understanding of the word. You've been listening, so you got these rules right here. You got these Ten Commandments you must follow. I was afraid of spending the rest of my life not in line with what god was calling me to be.

For example, as a child, I had always felt like I was blessed with the gift of healing. I would never let that leave me. So, even into my adult years, I continued to do that. But then people would say they didn't want me laying hands on them if I was some kind of lesbian because I couldn't possibly be full of the spirit. I'm full of the devil. So, I went through this whole conflict between me and god. I felt like healing had been something that was given to me. It was a call on my life but yet I could not feel comfortable with laying my hands on people who were going to think that I was possessed with this demonic spirit of lesbianism. So I began doubting myself and having these nightmares where I was being attacked by dogs. Each time this dog would be leaching on to me. It was a weird experience and I had those dreams for years.

Judgment
"How dare I sit in anybody's establishment and criticize these people based upon earrings and pants."

To Tania, a key part of her journey has been self-reflection. She feels that her willingness to take a critical look at herself and her behaviors has been just as important to her transformation as her willingness to think critically about religion and the church.

I would just tremble at the thought of the god of the Old Testament who is just so judgmental and envious and greedy that he needed the people to be controlled in some aspect. I didn't see him as being the loving and compassionate person that Jesus was. Jesus is supposed to be his only begotten son but yet they seemed to me to be totally different people.

Sometimes, I feel so guilty because so many of the people I used to associate with were mean. And I was mean. We were just so judgmental. If I saw a woman at church and she had lipstick on, I would just automatically think that she was going to hell because that just wasn't something that apostolic women do. If she had on some little dainty earrings, by the fact that she was wearing jewelry I had already had in my mind that she wasn't following god's word. Or if she had on pants, you knew she was going to be the talk of the town because everybody was going to let it be known that that is not of god. "Women don't be wearing pants."

You would also get a lot of flack from visiting another church without your pastor's permission. Oh yeah. Because now you would be dabbling in another kind of denomination that may be contrary to the way that the pastor's trying to lead you. I had a church that was transitioning into being nondenominational and they would allow their saints to wear pants. When I first went there, I'll tell you, I was shaken. The whole church was going up in flames as far as I was concerned. "Y'all got pants on, jewelry on, makeup on, too much lip gloss, too much this and that!" I was basically sitting there thinking that the whole church was going to burst into flames. But then, as I sat there and began to get into the spirit—at the time I was really just feeling the whole emotion aspect of it—I began to cry. I thought, *Wow. I can't believe how judgmental I just was. How dare I sit in anybody's establishment and criticize these people based upon earrings and pants.* To think that our god is just that jealous or that vengeful that he would just send this woman to hell even though to me she seemed to be exemplifying all that Christianity is about. To think that she was going to miss out on the kingdom just based on my church.

Money Issues
"God was sitting right there and... we were going like a tug-of-war."

As part of her deep desire to be a fully committed and devoted Christian, Tania gave so much money to her church that it had significant detrimental effects, both financially and emotionally, on her daily life.

In my experience with money, I went through a lot of guilt. I would be torn because I would wonder how I was supposed to explain to the light company that I had had the money but then went to church on Sunday and my pastor, my leader, told me that if I didn't trust god enough to pay my tithes then I was going to be punished for that. So, a lot of times I would be so conflicted by that. I would have the money in my Bible and my intentions were that I was going to pay my tithes on Sunday, but then I would get a notice in the mail about a disconnect and I would be really torn. I was fearful and very guilty. I would just be crying sometimes and I'd say, "Lord, I really need this money and I'm scared." I would be literally sitting in church and it would be like god was sitting right there and he's reaching for the money and I'm trying to hold on to it. We were going like a tug-of-war. And that's how I felt with my leader, my pastor. Like we're at a game of tug-of-war. And so I began to doubt god. I'd say, "Okay, if you don't help me, if I don't come up with this money in time, Imma be in the dark." It just set up a lot of fear and doubt in me. I'm going back and forth with god about this money.

But the thing is, there may not be just one offering. Sometimes it might get up to two or three offerings. He might say, "If you got a $100 bill, get in the $100 line. Hold on! Hold on! God's speaking. He's speaking it to me. Okay, listen to me. Listen now. He's feeding into me. There's a $300 line, a $500 line, and a $1000 line." They want you to get in these lines because supposedly the more money that you plant—they call it a seed offering—the bigger your harvest will be. You'll reap more than you can handle. Well, at times, I've done that and I have just been at a loss because I didn't come up with the money in time to pay the bill. I would feel so bad. And then they would say, "That ain't nothing but the devil talking." So even though sometimes I felt angry with god because he didn't make good on his promise, I was going to sacrifice because I wanted to be obedient. It's all about obedience to your pastor, your church, and to god. It was all about obedience. So I felt I was being obedient.

Coming Out of Two Closets
**"Now I'm going to hell because, not only am I a lesbian,
but I stepped away from god's word."**

Being both a lesbian and a freethinker has created quite a bit of turmoil for Tania. Coming from such a conservative and strict religious background, Tania has found it difficult to get her family to fully understand her opinions and feelings about life. Though she doesn't call herself an atheist, preferring to refer to herself as a freethinker, the concept of freethought is still too controversial for her family. Tania's freethinking tendencies and sexual identity have placed her firmly in the "outsider" category within her family.

About being a lesbian, my friends were really understanding because I just said directly to them, "I have this terrible weight on me and I just have to let you guys know. Even though it might jeopardize our friendship, I at least felt compelled to let you know." But they didn't really care. It didn't really bother them too much. But now the friends who I had taken to church a few times and taken to Bible study, those were the ones who were like, "Oh yeah! You tripping now! You done fell off the deep end now!" Of course, a lot of people are quick to blame your partner at the time, thinking that maybe they have a certain amount of control over you. So, not only are you possessed but they're possessed, too.

When I was a kid and my father ended up getting incarcerated again, I went to stay with a couple in the church and their family. Telling them was very difficult for me. The moment the mother found out that I was gay, she didn't even want me to come to her daughter's wedding. She thought that maybe I would be a bad influence at the wedding. So, one day my sister just told me, "Mom said you can't come to the wedding because you are gay." And I was just like, "Wow! Are you serious?" They thought that I was just going to come there and spread a demon of homosexuality and everybody was going to be passing out and throwing up this demon of homosexuality. I don't know what they were thinking. But, yeah, it just hit me like a knife. *Are you serious? I can't come to my own sister's wedding because of my lifestyle?* To this day, if I'm on the phone with them, they'll try to throw in a scripture or say something like, "Oh, why don't you just pray," like they are hoping that something will just touch me and I'll shout "Hallelujah! Thank you Jesus! I'm free!" But, I still love them unconditionally. Even though they are not my birth siblings, they had such a profound impact on my life.

I can't really discuss my feelings about religion with them because they feel that I'm just trying to adjust god's word to conform to the lifestyle I've chosen. So, even if I bring up certain questions, if I am trying to talk about my feelings and questions to my siblings or my friends or to anybody still deeply in the ministry, to them, I am questioning god's will and questioning god's word. And we've always known from the beginning: you don't question god. It just is what it is. I didn't even realize that it was okay to question god until I got older and I had this epiphany. But in their opinion, anything that I ask that's not in the traditional way that the church would have you believe, then I am trying to change god's word. Therefore, they'd say I really really have issues. It's one thing to be a lesbian but when you go trying to change god's word, then you really got some serious problems and I'm really going to suffer the repercussions from that.

Sometimes when I try to talk to people, they look at me and say, "You're weird." And I say, "Naw. I'm just a freethinker." I don't need you to agree with everything, but I just need you to listen and at least be willing to come up with your own understanding rather than to just keep saying,

"Well, what does the Bible say? What does the Bible say?" I know what the Bible says and I know what god supposedly said to somebody two thousand years ago. But don't you think that maybe the people who did the translating had their own motives in there somewhere? Some things just don't add up. But if I were to say, "Well, god told me something different," it's like, "Honey, god ain't tell you that. It's something wrong with you. You better call the pastor and see if you can get somebody to lay hands on you." That's the only answer I get. I need to intercede in prayer. I need to fast. I need to ask god to deliver me. But those same people can't explain to me why we have different laws under Christianity instead of all of the Old Testament laws or why we still have so much conflict in the world. Nobody's fasting about that. But the minute you find out that I'm a lesbian, you're ready to pull out the crucifixes and the holy water. They're not leading by example to show me compassion. Now people just live such contradictory lifestyles from what the Bible says and I'm just really fed up with the whole situation. I stepped away from it. But of course, to my family and acquaintances, I'm going to hell because, not only am I a lesbian, but I stepped away from god's word. But that's man's word. To me, it's not god's word.

Problems
"But yet they're still not at peace."

Far be it from Tania to give anyone a set of rules, beliefs, or opinions that she thinks are best. True to her chosen name, Journey, and her freethinking philosophies, Tania wishes that people would take the time to fully evaluate their religion, beliefs, morals, and desires and draw personal conclusions. She believes that this will help people find more peace in their lives.

I don't like to use the word "brainwashing," but people aren't allowed to be freethinkers. It's just mind manipulation. It's not that I was very angry, but I was disappointed at how much hatred and discrimination people had toward one and other, all based upon the Bible. So, okay, even after two thousand years and after god spoke to Moses and Elijah and all these people, is he incapable of speaking now? Why hasn't he spoken to anyone in over two thousand years? And why do we constantly go back to this old document? People think that one day god is going to show up and have his judgment. So, people continue to do all these things and follow the strict rules of the church, but yet they're still not at peace. When you talk to them at work or at the office or when you talk to them at the grocery store, they're still struggling. They're hurting and just waiting on god to do something different in their lives, but really it's because they're looking at this man that's telling them, "Follow me. Follow me. This is the way to salvation." And he's constantly going inside their pockets when he already knows that your salvation is within you. He already knows that. But if he tells them that and people start to stray away from the church, then what does that do for his income? Then how is he going to afford all his bills. How is he going to pay his mortgage if people really knew that the only concepts to life are to love yourself, to love others as you love yourself, and to do unto your neighbors as you want done unto you. They're just laws of the universe. But because of the mind manipulation, people think, "If I don't do this or if I don't do that or if I don't follow this person then I'll be the outcast." And when you speak out against that, you're considered to be demonic. But really, you don't have to follow anything but your soul, your own personal relationship and spirituality.

7

ON PHYSICAL HEALTH

"Beseeching Him that He Would Come and Heal"
—Luke 7:3

Black women find themselves in the unfortunate position of being the most religious and devout demographic in the country while disproportionately suffering from some of the most horrendous yet preventable diseases. Based on the teachings of the church, these women should be some of the healthiest people because of supernatural blessings. These statistics tell the sad truth. Black women need to realize that not only do their supernatural beliefs and yearnings *not* help them but that their beliefs also often create a breeding ground for unnecessary suffering. The statistics are gloomy.

Sexually Transmitted Diseases/Infections

According to the Centers for Disease Control (CDC), black women are much more likely to contract a sexually transmitted disease (STD)—specifically, chlamydia, gonorrhea, or syphilis—than any other demographic. How many times more likely? Table 1 shows the actual number of cases of these STDs per 100,000 people by demographic.

Table 1. Number of STD Cases per 100,000 People by Demographic

	White Males	White Females	Hispanic Males	Hispanic Females	Black Males	*Black Females*
Chlamydia	84	270.2	237.7	788.8	970	*2,095.5*
Gonorrhea	21.5	32.8	54.5	63	555.2	*557.5*
Syphilis	3.9	0.4	8.1	0.6	31.3	*8.2*
TOTAL	109.4	303.4	300.3	852.4	1,556.5	*2,661.2*

Source: CDC, "Sexually Transmitted Disease Surveillance, 2009," tables 11b, 21b, and 34b, http://www.cdc.gov/std/stats09/.

Based on these figures, black females are twenty-five times more likely to have chlamydia and twenty-six times more likely to contract gonorrhea than white males, and they are more than twenty times more likely to have syphilis than white females. Even within the black community, black women are 70 percent more likely to contract one of these three STDs than black men.

HIV/AIDS and Sexually Transmitted Diseases

The HIV/AIDS rates in the black community are equally astounding. According to the CDC,

- The rate of new HIV infections for black women was nearly fifteen times higher than for white women and four times higher than for Latina/Hispanic women.

- At some point in their lifetimes, an estimated 1 in 30 black women will be diagnosed with HIV/AIDS.

- HIV/AIDS was the ninth leading cause of death for all blacks and the third leading cause of death for both black men and black women aged 35–44.

- The presence of certain sexually transmitted diseases/infections (STD/Is) increases a person's chance of contracting and transmitting

HIV. Since black women lead the nation in cases of STD/Is, they are at a greater risk of contracting HIV/AIDS than most other groups.[1]

As these statistics make clear, the HIV/AIDS epidemic is presently ravaging the black community. The effects are far-reaching and have a profound affect not only on those who are infected but also on the broader community. Just consider the implications of its effects in the 35–44 age range, when people are stabilizing their careers, buying homes, and raising families.

The STD/I statistics for black women are mind-bendingly appalling! Why are black women two, eight, ten, and even twenty-five times more likely than other demographics to become infected with almost every one of the most prevalent STD/Is? Traditionally, the black community has been known for its strict mores governing sexual activity. Heterosexual activity between a married couple is the only kind of sex that is acceptable. Period. There's no need to have an open conversation about sex. After all, why have a dialogue about the various types of sex that are considered sinful? Educating about sex, teaching about the use of birth control and condoms, and considering alternatives to intercourse, such as masturbation, are complete taboos. The thought is that talking about these matters could only help unmarried people sin, or in some instances, help married people sin, too. And the church does not want to be an accessory to sin.

These kinds of prohibitions obviously exist outside of the Black Church. The Catholic Church has been castigated in recent years for discouraging the use of condoms in African nations. Evangelical Christians, regardless of race and ethnicity, have notorious reputations for withdrawing their children from public school, opting instead for homeschooling because they do not want their children exposed to sex education. In recent years, we have even heard politicians chime in and decry the use of masturbation as a way to promote abstinence. Clearly America's hang-ups about sex extend far beyond the walls of the Black Church, but that does not change the fact that the Black Church promotes a message about sex that has not been helpful for black women and has been, in many ways, directly detrimental.

Obesity

It is my opinion that the most alarming statistics regarding the health of America's black women are in reference to how many are overweight and obese. The Behavioral Risk Factor Surveillance System (BRFSS) data collected from 2006 to 2008 by the CDC reveals the following statistics:

- More than one-third of all blacks (35.7 percent) are obese. Obesity is defined as having a body mass index greater than or equal to 30.

- The prevalence of obesity in blacks overall was greater than in any other racial or ethnic group surveyed. It is 51 percent greater than in whites.

- Nearly four in ten black women (39.2 percent) are obese.[2]

As further support to the thesis of this book, the most obese regions in the United States, the South and Midwest, are also the most religious.

The National Health and Nutrition Examination Survey (NHANES) often finds a higher prevalence of obesity overall than does the BRFSS. For example, the 2003–2004 NHANES found that 45 percent of all blacks were obese,[3] while the 2007–2008 NHANES found that

- More than three-quarters of black women (78.2 percent) are overweight or obese (BMI 25+).

- More than one-quarter of black women (27.9 percent) had BMIs greater than or equal to 35 (obese).

- One in seven black women (14.2 percent) had BMIs greater than or equal to 40 (morbidly obese).[4]

Let that sink in: nearly four out of five black women are overweight or obese, nearly one in three are obese, and one in seven are morbidly obese. These rates are two, three, and four times greater respectively than almost every other demographic!

The NHANES data was collected by having survey workers directly take the measurements, while the BRFSS data was self-reported. This means that the NHANES survey—which has the more startling statistics—is more likely to paint an accurate picture.

Lifestyle-Related Illnesses

Women, regardless of race or ethnicity, have led the nation in cardiovascular disease (CVD)–related deaths since 1984. And, as usual, black women specifically have the highest rates of these preventable causes of death. According to the American Heart Association and American Stoke Association,

- Out of every 100,000 black women, 277.4 will die every year as a result of cardiovascular disease.
- Black women have the highest rate of death from stroke in the nation.
- Nearly half (45.7 percent) of all black women, age 20 and older, have high blood pressure (HBP).
- Black women are 2.6 times more likely than white women to die from HBP-related problems.
- The overall rates of heart failure, diabetes, and death from diabetes in black women more than doubles that of white women.[5]

Judith Stern, professor emeritus in the Department of Nutrition at Univeristy of California–Davis, once said, "Genetics loads the gun, but environment pulls the trigger." I include that quote because, not only do black women appear to have high levels of satisfaction with their bodies,[6] but they also seem to accept their poor health as a fact of life. This is in part because their mothers had diabetes or heart disease; their grandmothers had it; and they believe they are likely to end up with it, too. The black community tends to believe that black women are just naturally bigger than women from other races. Black women are usually proud of their "big booties" and they like being "thick." What some call "fat" (sizes 10, 12, 14+), black women call "thick." More and more black women see "love yourself" campaigns that tell them that it is okay to be "big and beautiful." While the premise that we need to love ourselves no matter what we look like is meaningful, it doesn't mean that we should be complacent. Self-esteem and self-image are very different from physical health. We should be bolstering our self-esteem and self-image by doing what is good for our health. When we are physically healthier, we usually experience an increase in mental health, self-esteem, and self-image.

So what does the Black Church have to do with the grim health statistics of black women? The Black Church and the Bible explicitly or implicitly endorse messages such as:

- Exercise is not important. "Bodily exercise profits little." 1 Timothy 4:8
- You can eat anything you want. Despite the fact that the Old Testament prohibits certain foods, people sometimes use the story in Acts 10 to justify eating anything, even unhealthy foods.
- Members should depend on faith and prayer for healing.

The Black Church also creates an environment and fosters an attitude that might hinder a woman's ability to focus on her physical and mental health. Sometimes, the church intends to foster a strong community through social functions, but it rarely espouses ideas or holds events that promote healthy behaviors and increase mental health. For example, members are told that they should attend church every time the doors open and frequent social gatherings, which are often centered around food.

Although there are a myriad of other factors that contribute to the poor health of black families—lack of money, poor access to healthcare, food deserts, etc.—the church's impact on the issue is undeniable. Consider the social part of being a member of a church. Just like families, black churches require a high degree of commitment. That commitment means that the more devout women find themselves in church three, four, five days a week. When adding that level of commitment to church to other commitments like jobs and families, when are these women supposed to find time to dedicate to self-care activities? The Black Church prides itself on placing god above all things and the belief is that a person demonstrates that commitment by what you *do* for the church. Therefore, it is easy for black women to simply disregard other important issues in their lives and prioritize themselves low on their to-do lists.

Also, black churches have traditionally failed to educate their members on proper nutrition and the importance of a healthy lifestyle. Black churches are known for their fish fries, anniversary dinners, and regular after-service gatherings at local all-you-can-eat buffets. Poor eating habits and unhealthy lifestyles learned in a woman's primary family are now reinforced by the only institution stronger than the black family. Excuses like "You gotta eat" and "God will bless the food to make it healthy" are used to excuse behaviors that everyone already knows are unhealthy.

The single most egregious contribution of the Black Church to this health crisis is its teachings regarding the dependence on and power of prayer. Prayer is the panacea that is supposed to take care of everything. Ironically, health and healing tend to be the most frequent prayer requests. Everything from a headache to stage-four cancer is believed to be cured by prayer. Black women are instructed to prayer over unhealthy meals. They are expected to pray for their sick babies. They are trained to lay hands on themselves and anyone else who might be sick. Combine this thinking with the socioeconomic problems facing black women and you have a disaster waiting to happen. When poor black women do not have insurance or money to go to the doctor, they are likely to ignore the problem and simply pray and hope for the best. Often, there are community clinics that people can go to for free or low-cost treatment, but black women will even ignore those opportunities in favor of prayer.

Black churches have traditionally and insidiously linked suffering with godliness. If a person can suffer through an illness depending only on prayer, it is believed to be a sign of their great faith. If they are sick, there must be some greater divine purpose or some spiritual lesson to learn. Unfortunately for people under this spell, their health suffers. The irrational dependence on prayer becomes painfully and regretfully obvious when one considers the many cases of children who die every year because their parents depend on faith healing. While this happens in all kinds of churches and denominations, not just in black churches, the results are the same for black women as they are for those poor, neglected children. But no one keeps track of adults who die—or practically kill themselves—because they stubbornly refuse to address the real issues.

Sadly, black women are disproportionately affected by poor health and preventable disease. The Black Church is partially responsible for black families' disregard of scientific research and evidence and for the mistrust of medical professionals that is common in the black community. A failure to provide or support real sex education, a failure to emphasize the importance of quality diet and exercise, and an inordinate focus on the power of prayer to heal all problems are all faults of the Black Church. Sometimes, physicians and other health professionals are even overtly denigrated in the church because they are believed to be part of some sort of nefarious establishment intent on destroying Christian faith. Preachers may say things such as, "The doctor might be smart, but he's not smarter than god! We know something the doctor doesn't know. We know the power of prayer!" Seemingly innocuous comments like this plant themselves deep into a person's thought processes. The next time a woman who listens to those words gets sick, she will hear them echoing in her mind.

When you take many of the explicit words of black Christian ministers, various Bible verses, and implicit expectations that black women be devout Christians who give all of their time and energy unquestioningly to the church, it is not hard to see why black women compose one of the most unhealthy demographics in the United States.

8

IVORI'S STORY

Childhood Experiences
"Honestly, I blame my skepticism on my mother."

Ivori is a twenty-seven-year-old woman who was born and raised in the Midwest but currently lives in the South. Although she attended Catholic schools, she was never really indoctrinated with religious beliefs.

I did not grow up in a very religious household. My parents weren't churchgoing people. My dad's from Mississippi and my mom's from Alabama and both of them grew up with a Baptist upbringing. I was born in Chicago and that's where I was partially raised until I was twelve. My parents put me in a Catholic private school until the sixth grade. However, I was never forced to go to church. Honestly, I blame my skepticism on my mother. Although my parents did put me in a Catholic religious environment, she always taught me to think for myself and question nearly everything. So, she did me a pretty good service with putting me in supposedly a better school but at the same time teaching that if this doesn't make sense, find out why. Questioning everything and thinking about everything can be good or bad because it can drive you nuts. But there were no messages like, "Ivori, you need to pray or you need to get right with god." You know, all of the sayings that holier-than-thou Bible-thumpers would throw out.

An Adult Experience
"This is where I belong. This is what I've known from birth."

As a lot of people who did not grow up in very religious homes do, Ivori had a longing for some kind of spiritual connection. In adulthood, she made the decision to seek out a Catholic church with which she could fellowship. And, for a while, she found a measure of peace and satisfaction there.

Three or four years ago I got baptized. I was finding myself. I guess I started looking for answers. And I've attended several different denominations of churches throughout the city, but since I did attend Catholic school through the sixth grade, I'm assuming that that's why I'm most comfortable there. They weren't as judgmental as Protestant churches. And, of course, they only go to church for exactly an hour. It seems as if everything made sense when I would sit in that building and listen to the music and the sermon.

For adults, there's a program called RCIA, Rites of Christian Initiation of Adults. I was twenty-three or twenty-four years old and for the first time, I was baptized. I had been attending night classes to make sure that it was what I wanted to do. There was no pressure. They said, "At the end of the program, after taking these notes, after taking these classes and asking these questions, if you decide this is not what you want to do, then that's fine."

And it was actually a very smooth process. You'd go to optional classes and get to ask questions after service. I even connected to one of the few black families. Everything made sense. This was where I belonged. This is what I've known from birth. I felt as if I had found a church home. And honestly—I doubt this would ever happen—but if I were to revert back to Christianity, I would go back to the same faith and the same church. But I'm sure it's pretty hard to go from agnosticism and atheism back to a belief because once you know, you always know.

It's kind of funny because when I see the church members who encouraged me and guided me through this process, they probably want to ask why I don't go to church anymore. And of course I can't say, "I don't believe that anymore. I don't believe what you believe." They won't accept it. But maybe going through that process actually helped me come to terms with my lack of belief. In the midst of going to church, that's when I realized that this is crap. There's a large following to this crap. That was around the time I started to research atheism and I was very delighted to find that there were people like myself on Facebook. I was like, "A Black person! Yes!"

The Problem with Prayer
"I've never prayed for myself."

Despite having had a great experience in her Catholic church, Ivori still came to the realization that she simply did not believe. Her deconversion started as a simple epiphany. Afterward, the process of leaving the religion behind was relatively easy.

What took me away from religion and faith as a whole was prayer. I've always been told that if you pray, things will happen. *Ask and ye shall receive.* One day, I was in the living room and I realized that I've only been praying for the same two things all my life and I'm supposed to get them because I wanted them with all my heart.

I've never prayed for myself. I've been praying for two things: make my dad a better person and heal my mother of her diseases. The same two things for twenty-seven years! And I was in my living room and I stopped. *Why am I praying? These are either going to happen or it's not. There's nothing I can do about it. I can't force my dad to be a better person. I can't heal my mother of her diseases.* So, it hit me like a ton of bricks. I said to myself, "Ivori, you are agnostic. You don't believe half this shit. Prayer does not work!"

I never really questioned the Catholic Church, the priests, the pope. Them raping people, that never really resonated and it didn't have anything to do with my deconversion. It had nothing to do with that. It had to do with Christianity as a whole.

Relationships
"I'm certain that religion is going to come up on the first date and what am I going to say?"

Black women in general complain about the difficulties of finding and keeping quality, meaningful relationships. Ivori's experiences with relationships were impacted by race when she was attending church and by her lack of religion once she was out.

The Catholic Church that I attended was mostly white. And these were white people with money. So, needless to say, it would be frowned upon if they dated a black woman, especially a black woman without money. People are always saying black women won't date white men, but in my experience, it's been the other way around. White men won't date black women. I don't know if it's that they're just not attracted to black women or if they're afraid of rejection or if it's just that we don't have the European standard of beauty. I just don't know. So, that contributed to me not dating in the church. Now, coming out of the church, being an outcast, so to speak, I don't really look for relationships right now. And I guess this is my own close-mindedness, but I'm certain that religion is going to come up on the first date and what am I going to say? "I'm an atheist." And what are they going to say? "Check please!" And so I guess it's my own fear that I'm not going to be accepted for who I am. And I'm not going to lie and say I believe what they believe because eventually it's going to come up.

Labels
"This is something that I'm struggling with."

Like many new black nonbelievers, Ivori struggled with the self-labeling process. At the time of the interview, she maintained that she was agnostic due to its most basic meaning—"without knowledge." She struggled with the connotations of various terminology and her perceptions of the people who held such labels. Since the time of this interview, Ivori has taken the label of atheist.

I label myself agnostic. I know that you can be an agnostic atheist but I have not put a definitive answer on whether or not I believe. I believe that it's possible that there might be a higher being, but, honestly, I don't know and this is something that I'm struggling with. I'm leaning more toward, *No, I don't believe in a higher being,* but then I do think that there might be something higher than us. I'll tell you, I'm only semicloseted right now. Maybe in a few years down the road, I'll say, "I don't care what you know or what you think about my religious views." So, right now, I'm semicloseted and I'm leaning more toward getting out of the closet. But, of course, you know, for several factors, it's not easy for some.

Problems with the Church
"What kind of people are they breeding in these buildings?"

Although Ivori never attended a historically black church and has not been a part of that culture and those norms, she's experienced enough through visiting black churches, heard enough through friends, family, and associates, and seen enough through pure and simple observation to express concerns about how she feels religion is negatively impacting the black community.

Blacks tend to be very, very conservative considering our history. Overall, we vote Democratic, which tends to lean to the left and be more liberal, but we're actually very conservative. For example, we're homophobic. Considering our history, we should be the last people to judge. But we take on this close-minded stance. It's very divisive. From the outside looking in, they seem okay with being divisive because it's ingrained in them. They're indoctrinated with it. If you set foot in a black church, they'll turn around to see what you have on. And they say, "Come as you are," because they say that's in the Bible, but they don't really mean that.

One big thing I have a problem with is homophobia. They just think that gays are disgusting. When they began to recognize civil unions, my uncle's wife, who's a very fundamentalist Christian, said, "This is such a waste of time because even if it's legal here, it's illegal in the sight of god." And I thought, *Open your mind! You could possibly have a friend that's gay. A gay person could save your life.* Also, I wait tables and black church people are the worst people to wait on. I mean, you just got out of church and you're pretty much being a butt hole. To me, that says a lot about your character. What kind of people are they breeding in these buildings? What kind of people are you sending out into the world? What messages are you teaching that you're sending these hateful people out into the world?

I don't go out much. I'm a loner anyway but I live in a small city. And that's pretty much why I'm single. Try being open-minded in a small city in the Deep South. Most of them are really churchy and don't want to be open-minded to anything else. For example, when we lived in Chicago, I remember very distinctively they would ask, "Do you go to church?" Not assuming that you're a Christian or that you go to church. But when you come to the South, they ask, "What church do you go to?" So, the black community within itself is divisive, but then the southern black community is even more divisive.

Michael Baisden, a radio host who I follow on Facebook, once asked: "What would you do if you found out the next day that god was not real?" I read the posts. About 97 percent of them used the phrase: "I don't want to entertain that thought!" That's just amazing that they don't even want to question it! I have a thirst for knowledge and it's that thirst for knowledge that drives you to question more, to want to see more. There are always two sides to every coin, but we don't even want to question it.

9

RAINA'S STORY

Childhood Experiences
"I had experiences in mixed churches, but primarily the ones that I wanted to go to were black."

Raina is a twenty-seven-year-old woman whose childhood was not overly religious. With a mother who did not attend church regularly, she was primarily exposed to religion through her grandmother and aunt. Raina recalls some good memories from her varied experiences with Catholicism and Protestantism.

My mother and my father were never married, but they are all fairly educated and have college degrees. My grandmother on my father's side used to take me to church a lot when I was younger. My mom is Catholic and my father's family is Protestant, but I had a Catholic christening. My mother was never particularly religious for most of my upbringing. I mean, my mother believed in God and my mother gave me a Bible but I pretty much read it on my own. She gave me little prayer books every so often. My grandmother and my aunt were primarily responsible for exposing me to religion.

Every summer I would visit my aunt because she didn't have a daughter. I was her surrogate daughter. Pretty much everything we did anytime I went to visit her in the summer was biblical. I was in church camp, church basketball, and in the church Bible study. Everything was Christian. We would go on these excursions to Christian bookstores and we had all of these Christian movies and video games. It was crazy.

The two Baptist churches I went to, they danced. One of them didn't speak in tongues and one of them did. In the Methodist church we didn't get exposed to a lot of that, you know. I always preferred the quieter services, though. The church that my aunt went to initially was a primarily black church. She ended up going to a multiracial mega church but it was primarily White. So, I had experiences in mixed churches, but primarily the ones that I wanted to go to were black. I mean, it's fine to go to white churches but the music sucks. I'm sorry!

One of the great things about black churches is the gospel music and the artistry, even the preaching, to a certain degree. In a white church they teach. I have to give it to them. They teach. The guy standing up there is teaching and he's not trying to stir you up. He might stir you up a little bit towards the end, but not really. Black church, I mean its pageantry. People are wearing crazy hats and the amens, hallelujahs, and the choir!

My grandmother used to take me on the weekends. It kind of gave my mom a break. The pastor that runs this particular church is really crooked. It didn't start out that way but my grandparents were just fed up with some of his practices. Like, he gets a salary of a hundred thousand dollars a year. He got some sort of Benz as a birthday gift. He wanted the church to not only raise his salary but he wanted them to pay for his kids' private school.

This church is in an economically depressed area. My grandparents did pretty well for themselves. But even if you didn't know the economic makeup of the church, some things are just going a little too far. And they felt that he's gone too far. So, they just stopped being associated with that church and they went to another one. But that pastor and his wife are everywhere and I still see him and his wife and I'm disgusted looking at him.

Teenage Religion
**"Usually there's this point where you hit this emotional high
and then you bring it back down."**

*Although her childhood religious experiences were pleasant, Raina says that,
as she got older, she became genuinely interested in religion. She recalls being
so indoctrinated that she even convinced her mother to get back into church.
Raina truly began to study her Christian beliefs because she had a strong
desire to understand and be closer to god.*

I pulled my mother into it. I knew, when I was about eleven or twelve,
that I needed to get baptized and, because I got baptized, I was telling my
mother about how important it was that she get baptized, too. I didn't
want her to go to hell. So my mother, because she's Catholic, never got
baptized. She was confirmed but not baptized. I didn't necessarily know
enough about the Catholic Church to think that her faith was bad. I
wasn't really thinking, *Oh my mother went through conformation.* I was
like, *My mother doesn't go to church.* So my mom started to go to church
with me.

I went to teen retreats to "acquire the fire." That's a mainstream
nondenominational Christian thing. Now that I'm older, I realize that
it really resembles a Nuremburg Rally because they don't really give
the kids any real sort of information. It's all propaganda, you know,
and manipulation. They know exactly what to do. They know how to
emotionally stir people up. It's the music. It's the words that you say. It's
how you plan your program so that you can get a vibe, an anticipation.
Usually there's this point where you hit this emotional high and then you
bring it back down. Then you tell them about god's redemptive power.
That's how you do it.

It's sad. I pulled my mother into religion because I was so desperate
to clear myself and make sure I wasn't going to hell. At sixteen, seventeen,
I was a Sunday school teacher. I was teaching five and six year olds,
teaching them the Apostles' Creed and things like that. But at that time,
I decided that the Trinity, at least, was BS because I couldn't find the
Trinity in the Bible anywhere. So it started. All the beliefs I had just

started to disintegrate. So I stopped going to church at about seventeen and I was agnostic for a number of years. I mean, a part of me never really bought it all. I figured out ways to kind of rationalize it all to myself. If the pastor said something I didn't agree with, I tried to figure out a way. "Well, maybe he's interpreting it wrong."

The Beginning of the End
"He encouraged me to read and I read myself out of the Bible."

Desiring to understand god more, Raina listened to her ministers and read everything she could find. But because of her love for reading, the more she learned about her beliefs the more she started questioning and doubting. When she read some of the more disturbing and egregious stories in the Bible about topics such as rape, Raina could no longer ignore her doubts.

Early on, I was still a child that was impressionable, but when I got about sixteen and seventeen, I started seeing the world not so much in black and white anymore. I started to realize that a lot of people try to scare you into seeing things a certain way. There were always these tracts to read, you know, *Our Daily Bread*, or other things. I mean, I loved reading and, as my mother realized I had a college reading level in the third grade, she was like, "Okay, well keep at it." I got a lot of things really early.

They always tell you, "Study to the show thyself approved." So I said to myself, "If reading the Bible takes me out of the Bible and god doesn't make any mistakes and god is truly leading me, then I should come back to god." That was my feeling. The Bible should bring me to a better understanding of god but, if it didn't, it meant that a lot of it was just about what people were telling you to believe. The last Methodist church I went to, that man was very intelligent and very considerate. He actually goes into the text. Most of the stuff that he was teaching came directly from the text. So, it was good and bad because here I am listening to him but I'm also reading. He encouraged me to read and I read myself out of the Bible.

So yeah, it was definitely all about putting that shit aside and saying,

"I can read it; I don't need your help!" I thought, *You're talking about slavery!* He's just standing there and I thought, *Wait a second, this woman got raped. What happened to the dude that attacked her?* It's like, *Did this fool really just kill his daughter? Why did God let him do that?* There were so many things that I was reading and it was almost like I was reading it for the first time. I would go to church and they would talk about people like Tamar or other stories and I had just never thought about it that way. That's when I woke up! That's when I woke up!

Yeah, there were all these things that I didn't believe in literally. I didn't believe in the literal Noah's Ark. I never believed that. It was a nice little story and, when I was a kid maybe, I did sort of believe it until I was old enough to know better. And when I thought about Adam and Eve, I was like, "I don't think it's possible that they populated the entire earth from just two people. And where the hell did Cain find his wife?" Some people would say, "Well, it must have been his sister." So then I'm like, "Why would he marry his sister? Why would god want it that way?" That's just stupid.

Early on, I didn't want to believe in evolution because I knew that atheists believed in evolution. I thought, *Maybe the atheists got it wrong but evolution has to be in there somewhere. If I could just explain it to them they'd understand.* But I still wasn't a six- day biblical creationist. Nobody ever taught me that. I was curious enough to value science but none of the adults that were in the church were knowledgeable or curious enough themselves to give the answers. So when it came to certain things, I felt it was okay to go to the science, especially if god didn't address it himself. I said, "Well, science can't be all bad if there are all these other good things that come from science." Because, you know, anything good has to come from god.

The last time I can recall, we went to a Catholic church on Christmas Eve. I hadn't been since I was a child. Sometimes they come through the crowds sprinkling holy water. I just remember catching some of the holy water on the back of my neck. Now, this is after I had come out as an agnostic and it was funny to me because it was so cold. And my mother and I were joking afterwards that the holy water was burning the demons out of me.

Fear and Nightmares
"The water was forbidden and I got swallowed up
by the earth every time."

Around the time that Raina started to become more invested in serving god, she began experiencing more religious fear. She recalls vivid dreams that haunted her for years.

I got my first Bible when I was about five. It was a kid's Bible and it had all types of pictures in it. I think the main reason I was driven to read that Bible was the stories. The Bible has some pretty great stories. I mean, it's not particularly well written but it has some pretty decent stories in it. That's why you can make a full-length feature film about Samson and it would be really entertaining. That's kind of where you are as a kid. You're like, *Wow, he killed somebody with a jawbone!*

So, that's where the Bible interest came from, but the fear started when I heard about hell and what was supposed to happen when you went there. The fear really started when I was maybe eleven, twelve, thirteen. I was absolutely fearful! First, I was reading the Bible to satisfy what my family was telling me to do. Then, I started reading it so that I could at least see for myself what they were talking about, like the Rapture and all that crazy shit. But it wasn't really coming from a place of scholarship. I wasn't really sinking my teeth in. It wasn't until I got older that I really got into it and started having nightmares. I actually had some weird dreams and there were people who were telling me that my dreams were messages from god and I should pay attention to them.

One was so vivid to me when I was kid. I think I was probably six or seven and I had it up until the time I was about twelve. I was a shepherd and I was very thirsty. I was always thirsty for some reason. So, I got to a well, a huge well the size of an ocean. There was writing on the well and you couldn't read it all because it was the size of the ocean. So, I just decided to just take a drink, but apparently the water was forbidden and I got swallowed up by the earth every time. It doesn't sound so bad when I put it like that now but in the dream it's terrifying. It was so real to me that I felt I could touch the water. It started particularly in times of stress. So my first thought was about hell and demons. Demons, they did scare me.

I had some dreams where I was just talking to someone. I couldn't see the face but this person was supposed to represent god or something. I had other dreams about the Crucifixion. As I got older, some of them were more comforting but I didn't really know how to contextualize them. So a lot of the time I just kept it to myself. I wouldn't say anything about it because people would tell me, "It's a message from god. You've got to take it as a sign."

I actually loved scary movies. Some of them really scared me, like *The Omen*, because at the end you say, "Oh my Gosh! This is real! This is going to happen in a few years!" Some of the demon movies were pretty funny and you just laughed at them because they were so clearly fictional. Other ones, especially the religious ones, kind of reinforced things and made you think.

God Is Always Watching
"People who don't believe in god or don't have the intention of going to hell will still go to hell."

Along with the nightmares that Raina experienced as a teenager, she was also worried about being under god's constant surveillance. Because of that, she policed her thoughts obsessively.

Eventually, I started to realize that, not only was god there, he's there all the time. I mean, I already knew that god is present if you went to church. So I could accept those times when you just fucked up and wasn't paying attention for some reason. But for him to watch all the time, that made me fearful. I'm like, "Everything I do? Everything?!" And I thought, *What if I didn't know that I was doing something wrong at the time.* I got various answers. Some people said it's really about the intention. Some people said it doesn't make a difference whether it's the intention or not. They said that people who don't believe in god or don't have the intention of going to hell will still go to hell.

The next thing that scared me was that god knew your thoughts. So not only couldn't I do anything, I couldn't even think about anything. That was terrifying to me. I would be like, "Put it away! Put it away! Put that thought away!" It got to a point where I was scared of almost everything, especially those things that were outside the church.

Sexuality
"It felt good. You enjoyed it. You didn't hurt anybody but you have to apologize for it."

Unlike many young religious people, Raina did not have much of an emotional struggle with the conflicts between religion and sexual activity. She had some minor periods of guilt but, by and large, she remembers having a sense of self-assurance that she could make responsible choices about sex. Therefore, she was not convicted by religious judgments.

When you are a kid, you start to explore your sexuality, you know. I remember my mother being very disturbed by that because her mother was very disturbed by it. I remember my mom had a major freak-out about it. I mean, I never had an issue with it because I felt that it was mine. I thought, *Besides, I'm not hurting anybody and I'm not even having sex.* Oh my gosh! It's so funny because this was sort of before I realized that god knew your thoughts and was there all the time. So, at a certain point I was like, *Okay! Well maybe if I just go under the blanket he'll look the other way.* And then at a certain point as a teenager I thought, *I don't do it very often. It's just this once.* So you slipped up and you pray like you're really sorry. It felt good. You enjoyed it. You didn't hurt anybody but you have to apologize for it. And we punish children for what's really a natural thing. As long as your kid is not masturbating publicly or doing it at inappropriate times, who's it really hurting? I just never understood that. But even though my mom freaked out about it, when I got older, I guess she kind of mellowed out a little bit. I think it was the age that bothered her because maybe she thought that if you start at a young age that means that you are going to be promiscuous.

I had a boyfriend when I was about fifteen and I'd seen all these girls in high school having relationships with these guys and they only had sex because the guys told them that they loved them or whatever. This was about the time when I started to fall out of religion anyway. So, I decided that I wasn't going to wait until I was married before I had sex. I said, "That's bull! I mean, do you ever buy anything without trying it first?" So I decided that, if I was going to have sex, I was going to have sex because I wanted to have sex. If god was going to ask me about it or punish me for it, I was going to feel good about my decision because it was my decision that I made for myself. It was not for my boyfriend and not for anybody else. It was because I felt like having sex.

So, I decided that I wanted to have sex and I didn't tell my mother. She was very hurt that I didn't talk to her about it first because she had talked to me about sex from the time I was five. But my friend, being the self-righteous person that she was at the time, decided that it was upon her to tell my mother that I did that. So, I actually had to see the disappointment in my mother's face as she realized that I was no longer a little girl. My mom said, "Okay. Well, were you at least safe? Who was it with? Was it with somebody that you at least care about?" When she realized who it was, she was like, "Okay. I kind of don't blame you now," because he was fine.

Family
"Let's not focus on the thing that we don't have in common. It's only one thing."

As with many black nonbelieving women, Raina went through several transitional phases as she slowly shed her religious beliefs. She found that her slow transition actually made it easier to discuss her changing beliefs with some family members, but there were others who disagreed with her at all stages. While she does not apologize for her lack of belief or shy away from discussing it, she says that she sometimes avoids the topic simply because she respects everyone's right to believe whatever they want.

My family knew when I decided I was agnostic. When I told my mother I was agnostic, she said the same thing I did to her when I was trying to get her to go to church: "I don't want you to go to hell." And she cried.

It was really sad and I felt bad that I was doing that, but, I couldn't help it. But my mom is cool with it now and it's so funny because my grandmother, the one who took me to church at 7:30 sunrise services for three hours and Bible study, she's agnostic now. When I was agnostic, I still believed that there was a Higher Power. I was calling myself agnostic, but back then I didn't understand what agnosticism was.

I think that I even believed that the god of the Bible was the god of everything else and it's just that we were imparting all of these other characteristics on him. I didn't feel like I needed the Bible or anything or anyone else to get into contact with god. Then I started reading up on these other religions and realized how improbable they were.

So, it was a slow process. I went from believing in the literal definition of god and Jesus to being a sort of a pseudo-Christian to calling myself agnostic. When I started realizing that the Christian ethic was still in my thinking, I started dismantling it and looking for another religion until I found that none of it was real. So, I went from that to being a full-on atheist. I am the only one in my family as far as I know.

My aunt was always of the mind that she was going to bring me back to the fold, even when I was agnostic. I haven't come out to her exactly, but I'm pretty sure she knows by now because my uncle knows. She's Catholic and her husband knows.

My father's side, they don't really care. They're all like, "Okay, you're still a good person. You're not out there killing people. You're in school getting an education. Good for you." My aunt is the more religious one out of my father's family and she just wanted to understand where I was coming from. So, she asked a lot of questions. We had a discussion and she was more open-minded. She goes to church but she likes some aspects of Buddhism. When I had the conversation with her, she was like, "So, you don't believe in god at all? Why don't you believe in god?" And when I told her, she said, "You know, I never thought about that before. I have to think about that for a while before I come back to you." My grandfather still believes in god but my grandmother says, "I don't know about it anymore." She watches a lot of history channels and I think that her enjoyment of history and the books that she's read have kind of gotten her to a point now where she believes it is probably more fiction.

But my uncle, for my birthday last month, he sent me a card. Now, he doesn't usually send cards. Sometimes he calls and sometimes he doesn't but I hadn't really gotten cards from my uncle in several years. So, last year I came out online and I pretty much told everybody that I was an atheist. He saw that on Facebook and wrote, "I understand that you don't believe in god any more but that doesn't mean that I'm not going to try to bring you back to god." Whatever! So, this particular birthday I get a card from him. Actually it wasn't even on my birthday and it was an e-card. I'm like, "You can't even send the e-card on the right day?" I opened the e-card and it's this really religious e-card. It was a prayer or something. And when it finished it was like, "I hope that god blesses you this year" and blah, blah, blah. I was sort of bothered by this because my uncle is not a particularly religious person. He's still Catholic, but I don't ever hear about him going to church. I never hear him talking about anything, you know? So, it offended me. So I wrote him a letter and said, "Okay, so now you choose to be self-righteous on my birthday about me. It's the one day that's about me and you decided to make it about you. I feel offended. Please don't do this again." I said, "I love and respect you and I would never do anything like that to you. Let's not focus on the thing that we don't have in common. It's only one thing, the belief in god. Everything else we have in common. We have the same values. We believe in the same things. We love each other. We value humanity. So, let's not make it about the one thing that we don't have in common, you know?"

He never responded, but I just wanted to let him know that I wasn't angry to the point that I just wanted to be done with him. I don't have enough family to just be discarding people, but I wanted him to be aware that I wasn't going to take that sort of behavior anymore. I mean, my aunt who is religious has sent me religious cards since I was knee-high to a grasshopper and I know she's not going to change, but for him to go from being the sort of uncle that sent cards sporadically, and none of them ever being religious, to going to sending all these religious cards was sort of fake to me.

This past Christmas I was home and my cousin said, "You're an atheist now. How does that work?" I was like, "It doesn't really. I am just an atheist. I don't have to do anything. It's not like I had a confirmation or anything. It doesn't mean anything different. I still have morals and I still believe in love, family, community, and all those sorts of things." And he said, "Oh, okay, that's fine."

I usually avoid posting stuff on Facebook because I understand that there are things that people can take out of context or take something that you say about religion or god personally. And without me being there, I can't explain to somebody that, by me thinking that religion is bullshit, it doesn't make them stupid. It's not something that I want to get into but actually Christians talk shit about other religions all the time. They talk shit about people who believe in a holy cow but say you can't take the name of god in vain. Come on! Even if I'm not directly attacking you, the fact that I have a view of your religion that's different from yours is a point of contention and I don't want that happening on my wall. On there I can't explain to someone directly, "Look, this is what it is. I'm not trying to hurt your feelings. I'm not trying to say that you need to change your life. If this is what's working for you, fine. But it's not for me."

My personal feeling is that if it's a lie then it's not good, but I accept your right to believe whatever it is that you want to believe as long as it doesn't affect me and you don't teach it to my kids. The thing for me is that, if you prove that something you say is true, I will spin on a dime! That doesn't mean that I'll worship it, but I would at least acknowledge that what you say has some validity. If you're an atheist, they think it means that you are closed-minded as though Christians are more open-minded.

The Biggest Problem
"The black woman is the one who is basically taking care of the family and making sure that all the family's needs are met even before her own."

Throughout the interview, Raina had some positive things to say about the Black Church. For example, she spoke highly of its ability to offer a supportive community and network at times. However, because of her belief that lies,

deceit, judgment, and shunning are always harmful, she believes that the
church's detriments almost always outweigh its benefits.

I think that a big problem in the black community is this homophobia.
Like it or not, homosexuals are us. They're the aunties and uncles that
you had in the family that never got married but had a "special friend."
Everyone has one story like that in the family and I think that's the
worst thing. We know we have them in our churches. They're our choir
directors. Some of them are our ministers. The church is so against them
and I think that's one problem for sure that I have with the Black Church.

I think the Black Church used to be more of a political mobilizing
force and did more in the community in terms of helping out other
people's needs. Some churches still do that very well, but this prosperity
gospel has got to go. It is not serving us at all. It's only serving those at
the top to fill their pockets and it's really distressing. So, I'm sorry. You
know I love my gay and lesbian family but I got to say that the prosperity
gospel is probably the main problem because people need to get their
needs met and stop thinking that they have to give their last dime to the
church. I saw an interview with Evander Holyfield talking about how,
if he had nothing left, he would still give his 10 percent tithes. That's
ridiculous! Especially when these people who are poor are convinced
that, if they give their tithes, they're going to somehow come into some
money. It doesn't make any sense. There's no economic model anywhere
that will support that and the church really needs to stop.

Ministers with jets and things, how do you own a jet and you know
that the majority of the people that are coming to your church are making
thirty thousand or less? These are not your typical ministers. Ministers
used to live in the church or live on the church property. Some ministers
used to even have to do their own maintenance on the church or had to
have side jobs just to make ends meet because they weren't there to get
rich. And the model has changed so that now it's time to get rid of the
prosperity gospel.

Thankfully, my mother was never that into the church but I had
friends. I have one friend right now whose mother goes to some church
where they preach the prosperity gospel. He actually studied in a seminary

but then dropped out. He doesn't want to be a minister anymore. He just wants to be a professor of theology, I think. And depending on what seminary you go to, you might actually study yourself out of the Bible. So, he was telling me that his mom was out of work or between jobs. She was having some hard financial times, but she needed a new car and she wanted this really, really nice car. Of course, she couldn't afford it but her minister told her that she needs to go ahead and get the really nice car so that she can show god that she was being faithful. My friend doesn't have a car for himself but now he's paying for his mom's car. It's like that with black women, especially, and we can't afford to make those sorts of bad decisions.

I mean, we could talk about the multimillion-dollar hair industry. Some black women are going way too far buying five thousand dollar weaves knowing that they can't afford it, but we are also doing way more than a lot of us are really obligated to do. I mean, think about any black woman in your family. You know that if somebody needs to get bailed out, if somebody needs college tuition, if somebody needs anything, who do they go to? They don't go to a man. They go to a woman because we know that, in our families, black women hold it down. He might be the one that is so called "in charge," but the black woman is the one who is basically taking care of the family and making sure that all the family's needs are met, even before her own. That's why our net worth is not what it's supposed to be compared to other races and men in this country.

I read an article that said that the average net worth of black women is a dollar or something crazy like that. Think about how many black women even know about a 401-K or who save anything every month. You know that, if they're saving at all, they're not really saving much, because they're giving it away. Sometimes you have to learn to be selfish, but for some reason black women have been raised to believe that they're not entitled to have anything for themselves and this belief gets reinforced in church.

10

ON SEX

"Thou hast played the whore also . . . because thou wast unsatiable; yea, thou hast played the harlot with them, and yet couldest not be satisfied."
—Ezekial 16:28

The Black Church is known for being one of the most sexually repressed and oppressive institutes in the United States. As Darrel Ray points out in his research about sex and religiosity, "Polls show that Blacks oppose abortion more fervently than any other group. Black Christianity is against homosexuality, masturbation, same-sex marriage, premarital sex, condom use, sex education and much more."[1]

A Lack of Education

Despite being among the most sexually conservative religious demographics in America, black women have among the highest rates of unplanned pregnancies in the country. In addition, while they represent only 13 percent of the female population, they receive 35 percent of all abortions.[2] Despite the Black Church's tough stance against premarital sex, according to the Annie E. Casey Foundation's 2010 Kids Count survey, African-Americans have the highest rate of single-parent homes, with 66 percent of black kids being born to unmarried mothers.[3] When you consider the evidence that only 13 percent of religious parents talk to their children about sex and that children raised with the most religion experiment with sex more than those raised with no religion,[4] it is no wonder that black women would be less prepared for healthy sexuality. As Ray points out, "People who are religious have a good deal of guilt about sex and sexuality but their behavior is about the same as the non-religious. Guilt is a key component of religious attitudes about sex but actual behavior, whether first masturbation, first oral sex, first intercourse, etc. do not change appreciably with religiosity."[5] Further, the focus on abstinence (and abstinence-only education) within the church and its community leads teens to educate themselves in other ways about sex.

As Ray found, despite strong opposition to pornography among religious groups, "porn . . . is a key source of sex education for religious teens. The most religious teens said they got their sex education from porn 33% of the time, the less religious 25.2% of the time."[6] As a result of this poor education, black women not only have the highest rates of unplanned pregnancies and abortions, but as discussed in chapter 7, they also suffer disproportionately from sexually transmitted diseases.

Singled Out

The statistics tell only part of the problem. Black women are also the ones who suffer the most when it comes to sexually based religious restrictions and judgment, forms of repression not easily identified or measured. In *Sexuality in the Black Church*, Kelly Brown Douglas writes: "The manner in which Black women are treated in many Black churches reflects the Western Christian tradition's notion of women as evil and its notions of Black women as Jezebels and seducers of men. For instance, there are still Black churches that require women to cover their legs with a blanket when sitting in a pew so they will not distract men. This excuse that Black women are too sexually distracting is also commonly used to keep these women out of the pulpit and ordained ministry."[7] According to Douglas, it is unwed black mothers who suffer the most:

In many Black churches unwed mothers are publicly chastised and made to repent in front of the whole congregation while the fathers are often ignored. This humiliating sexist ritual harks back to early Black church expectations that Black women should remain chaste after joining the church, a church that all the while said nothing about the sexual conduct of Black men. This double standard is hauntingly reminiscent of the logic used by White men who fathered children by Black women during the antebellum and postbellum period. These men were not held accountable for these children, who were seen as the sole responsibility of the mother because, according to White logic, it was the seductive, passionate manner of the Black women that caused the sexual encounter.[8]

Homosexuality

As several of the personal stories discussed in this book attest, treatment of homosexuals and attitudes toward homosexuality continue to be a detriment to the black community in general and to black women specifically. Again, Douglas rightly points out, "Whether they are churchgoers or not, Black people often argue that the Bible makes clear that homosexuality is a sin. By invoking biblical authority they place a sacred canopy, a divine sanction, over their views toward gay and lesbian persons. This canopy renders homophobia practically intractable. The Bible becomes, then, a tool for censoring a group of people, in this case, gay men and lesbians."[9]

The vast majority of the black community's resistance to acceptance of homosexuals and homosexuality is based on religious arguments. Another insidious phenomenon in the black community is how black mothers are sometimes blamed for *creating* homosexual sons. Effeminate behavior is often assumed to be associated with homosexuality. Therefore, women who are raising their sons in fatherless homes are sometimes accused of not working hard enough to ensure that their sons are exposed to positive male role models. "The 'overachieving' Black woman becomes the scapegoat for the so-called emasculation of Black men."[10] As discussed in previous chapters, "strong" black women are damned if they do and damned if they don't.

Douglas makes a very interesting and unique observation about the role and effects of rap music on black sexuality. "In general, the 'in-your-face' manner in which rap music exposes the unhealthy views of sexuality present in many segments of the Black community—and not just the hip-hop reality—signals the urgent need for a sexual discourse of resistance."[11] She says that "this music indicates the need for a stringent religio-cultural analysis."[12]

While many religious leaders decry rap music and blame it for the promiscuous and sinful behaviors of young black men and women, no one considers that it might be an outgrowth of social oppression and unrest caused, in significant part, by the Black Church itself, which has historically had a chokehold on black sexuality and has attempted to eradicate any form of sexuality deemed sinful.

Submission as a Mentally Transmitted Disease

All of this is to point out just how sexually unhealthy the black community is. The Black Church is responsible because it imposes a number of rules and restrictions on black women that are oppressive, unnatural, and harmful. For example, submission is a popular topic in a lot of churches. Despite the fact that most black churches are run on a day-to-day basis by black women—and despite the fact that black families are primarily led by black women—these very same ladies are expected to suddenly bow their heads and remain subservient when a black man appears in their lives, be it a pastor or a husband. "Masculine moral worth is defined by the exercise of power and control over women, children, and other men."[13] Therefore, "The Judeo Christian regime of organized religion is far more proscriptive for women."[14]

Hebrews 13:17 admonishes Christians to submit willingly because, if they do not, something bad might happen to them: "Obey them that have the rule over you, and submit yourselves: for they watch for your souls, as they that must give account, that they may do it with joy, and not with grief: for that [is] unprofitable for you." Because this verse does not tell us exactly what might happen to us, ministers, pastors, leaders, and husbands are free to fill in the blank with their own fear-inducing punishments in an attempt to scare women into submission.

In addition to the shame black women may already feel about their bodies because of societal and religious messages, they may also feel especially helpless because they are told that they do not actually have control over their bodies.

- *"Wives, submit yourselves unto your own husbands, as unto the Lord. For the husband is the head of the wife, even as Christ is the head of the church: and he is the saviour of the body. Therefore as the church is subject unto Christ, so [let] the wives [be] to their own husbands in everything" (Ephesians 5:22–24).*

- *"Wives, submit yourselves unto your own husbands, as it is fit in the Lord. . . . But he that doeth wrong shall receive for the wrong which he hath done: and there is no respect of persons" (Colossians 3:18 and 25).*

While these verses above pay lip service to the idea that men are supposed to show a certain level of deference to and respect for their wives, the church often overlooks those parts of the verses. You may hear a minister mention those lines once or twice, but the vast majority of sermons on husband-wife relationships deal with how the woman is supposed to behave since, as Hebrews 13:17 implies, the husband is the one who watches over the woman's soul. For example, I have even heard 1 Corinthians 7:2–5 used as biblical support for husbands to have the right to force their wives to have sex even if the woman does not want to.

Nevertheless, [to avoid] fornication, let every man have his own wife, and let every woman have her own husband. Let the husband render unto the wife due benevolence: and likewise also the wife unto the husband. The wife hath not power of her own body, but the husband: and likewise also the husband hath not power of his own body, but the wife. Defraud ye not one the other, except [it be] with consent for a time, that ye may give yourselves to fasting and prayer; and come together again, that Satan tempt you not for your incontinency.

These verses suggest that marriage is primarily about sex and that spouses are supposed to "render due benevolence" (have sex) and not "defraud" each other (withhold sex). Because they do not have power over their own bodies, the spouse who does not want to have sex must submit anyway to the one who does. Once again, these verses sound as if they allow for fair treatment of men and women alike, but the biblical precedence on the treatment of women has already been set throughout the whole of the Bible. "Women are both powerful and powerless in many religious marriages. They are subordinate to their husbands but have the power and the obligation to control sex. Their sexual desire and gratification is seen as unimportant and maybe even evil."[15]

In recent years, as the number of female pastors and ministers is on the rise, it is becoming more common to hear female ministers preach about the egalitarianism these verses endorse. However, a few verses about treating women with a modicum of fairness cannot cancel out the authority over women given to men according to the Bible. Based on my observation, it seems that, in response to the growing number of women who stand up against the traditional understanding of submission, there has been an equal and maybe even more vocal response from women who believe wholeheartedly that submission is the best thing for their gender.

An Urgent Need for Change

Clearly, the Black Church has a lot to answer for when it comes to the sex-related problems plaguing the black community. Its unwillingness to address sexual development and education from a scientific and factual perspective directly contributes to the high rates of unwanted pregnancies and, as described in chapter 7, the high rates of sexually transmitted diseases and the HIV/AIDS epidemic. When the church constantly sends out the message that abstinence is the only way to behave before marriage and that complete submission is the only acceptable posture after marriage, it leaves parents and other community members in a precarious position when trying to offer a more comprehensive take on human sexuality. When the church and community refuse to directly address issues like rape, incest, and molestation, it forces victims into the shadows. The church and its community castigate and embarrass women who become pregnant outside of marriage. Even when church members pitch in to help these women, it is usually offered only after the women rededicate their lives to the lord. Such help is conditional and not charitable.

Depression, anxiety, self-doubt, self-blame, anger, and all manner of emotional turmoil fester in black women when they are not getting any real, practical, honest support or help from the Black Church. As Douglas insightfully points out, "It is not enough for Black church and community leaders to instruct our children to simply say no to sex, drugs, or other destructive behavior. The Black church and community must engage in a sexual discourse of resistance that empowers Black women and men to celebrate and to love their Black embodied selves."[16]

11

HEATHER'S STORY

Childhood Experiences
"You couldn't laugh because you would be laughing at god."

Heather is a thirty-two-year-old woman who is currently in the process of separating from her husband. As a woman who has known that she was a lesbian since her childhood, she tried, off and on, to live according to what she was raised to believe. As a child, she was taught many of the same scary and hate-filled stories and proscriptions to which most black women are exposed.

I'm from a predominantly black city. Now, it wasn't always like that but when we got the first black mayor, all the white people left. So I don't know if they left and took their agnosticism with them or whatever it was. But it seems like everyone believed in a god. You know. You rarely hear somebody talk about a Muslim god. It's always the Christian god, Jesus and everything. Since my mom and my dad weren't together, I stayed with my grandmother the majority of the time. And just like any good grandmother, she took her granddaughter to church. It was a Baptist church. Even before I could ever understand anything, I was already in the church, already in the system. So there was like really no hope. In the beginning, I enjoyed church for the most part. I thought it was cool. Sunday school was fun to me. I was pretty smart, at least that's what the Sunday school teacher said.

And after Sunday school, we would go upstairs to the regular church and that was boring, of course. The only thing that was really funny was the women catching the Holy Ghost. Now, that was hilarious! It was always funny to see the women jumping up and down and falling out. But you couldn't laugh because you would be laughing at god or committing blasphemy or something. But at six or seven years old, what the hell do you know about blasphemy? What I didn't like about being introduced to god at that time was that it seemed like just around any corner was something scary. One of the things was about hell and the rapture. Yeah, tell a child that at the age of six and seven. That's a real big scare tactic. What does a child have to look forward to? They're always afraid. They're afraid to do this; they're afraid to do that because you feel like you're going to die at any moment or god is always judging you. It's like you can't even have a free will. So, I didn't like that. I thought that sucked. It just keeps you scared.

In the beginning, my mom was cool for the most. But around the time that she lost her job at the mill—that was the big place to work, because if you got a job at the steel, you know you got it made—and had my brother, she just became crazy. I mean really. Whatever sickness she had just escalated and she was way more abusive, verbally abusive, all that stuff. When that's the only person you have to look after you, how can a god allow something like that to go on?

A Realization
"I said, 'Can I kiss you?' And surprisingly she kissed me instead of beating me up."

Despite her worry about the so-called sinfulness of homosexuality, Heather came to a place in her teenage years where she could no longer deny her sexual orientation. Despite having heterosexual relationships, she decided to begin exploring her sexuality further. The more she lived according to her true self, the more conflict she felt privately and internally.

I also liked females. I knew I liked them because, when I was a kid, about six years old, I went to go see *Purple Rain* and I thought Prince was cool.

But, I thought Apollonia was gorgeous and I had a thing for her. Matter fact, I had a thing for all of Prince's women—Vanity, Diamond. He just picked sexy women, in my opinion. So, yeah, I was around six years old and I knew I felt something funny when I saw these pretty women. But growing up in the black community, it was always told that's wrong, that's wrong. It was always derogatory toward homosexuals. And then, to add insult, they would throw the god thing on top of it. So now there's this other psychological thing. I might die at any time because I like women. So, I'm like, "Come on! What's up with that?" I didn't like that growing up.

When I was in high school, I always liked the upper-class girls. They carried themselves better and they were better looking to me. When I was sixteen, I had this boyfriend who worked at Subway. He was the manager. I was dating him and I remember we went out to this park and I saw this girl with her crew of girls. I just started thinking about her, thinking about us hanging out or whatever. We ended up becoming friends, some kind of way.

Being around her, I knew I liked her but I didn't know how to come across because she was a tough girl. I didn't know if she was going to kick my butt or what. I could have just said it but back then I just wasn't bold enough because of the stigma. One time, we happen to be in the same room and in the same bed with each other because I was spending the night. So after talking all night, I asked her. I said, "Can I kiss you?" And, surprisingly, she kissed me instead of beating me up. But after that, I kept thinking, *I'm not gay because I'm not gay. It's wrong to be gay.* So, it wasn't that I was gay; I just liked her. That's how I identified it. But I knew I liked women. I knew I wanted other girls but it was always low-key.

We only messed around maybe two or three times. I was a senior during this time and I was all happy that I finally got a girl I liked. But, she came to me one day, after avoiding me a little bit. She said she couldn't mess around with me anymore because she had a dream and she saw the devil and all this kind of bullshit. You know, I was hurt. I was like, "Damn!"

You know, it's typical, the whole god thing coming in messing up something. It is kind of unfortunate for people, at least back then, since the black community is so over-spiritual. A lot of people end up getting in relationships that they don't necessarily want to be in. I think girls and girls should be allowed to date and guys and guys should be allowed to date. I think it could prevent so much heartbreak.

Coming Out
"I was like, *Fuck it*. I wore a gay necklace that had the pride symbol."

Heather had the horrible and unfortunate experience of being outed as a lesbian before she wanted. But once she was out, she decided to be honest with herself and others.

When I was still in high school and I was a senior, everything was cool. I felt like I was on top of the world. Finally, I had some acceptance. I was cool. I messed around with girls on the side. I was actually doing well in school. And for the first time I was actually being liked. I was really cool with that and everything was going well until a rumor came out that I was gay. I thought, *I knew something was going to happen.* I was living life too well. Something had to happen to knock me down a peg or two. So when this came out, I was just devastated. I couldn't just own it at the time. It was a different time than it is now.

People were talking about me at schools I didn't even go to. I didn't even know them. I thought it was this girl who told. She was the only person I really talked to about it because we used to mess around. Unfortunately for my dumb ass, I fought her because I thought she was the one running around saying this. And I still regret that to this day. You know, I really don't know who the hell said it. Anyway, I got brought out the closet when I was a senior and I fought the girl trying to deflect the rumors off me. But the last week of high school I kind of owned it. I was like, *Fuck it.* I wore a gay necklace that had the pride symbol. I kind of dared somebody to say something because they knew I could kick ass. So nobody said anything.

Unfortunately, during that time, I should have had more guidance around. Somebody who could have told me, "Look, when you go off to college, this type of stuff is accepted." But I didn't have any of those types of influences.

I didn't tell my mom until I was in the military. I told her when I was nineteen. I was with the love of my life when I told her. She was like, "Well, that's your life." She was into religion but she was understanding. I didn't care, though, because I was in California. She couldn't whip my ass from there. She didn't really help, though, because every time something went wrong she'd say, "Well you know it's not right to be with a girl." But I just wanted to be out.

Military
"So I had to live a double life."

In hindsight, Heather believes that she only joined the military out of a sense of having no other options. While enlisted, she struggled emotionally and psychologically from fear that someone would discover her homosexuality.

I just ended up going off to the military, which was dumb in retrospect, because I just wanted to get away from my hometown, but I went to a place where they still don't like gays with don't-ask-don't-tell type stuff. You couldn't be gay in the military. Of course, in the military it is "under god" and that type of shit as well. You had those problems and the possibility of getting kicked out for being gay. So there was all this unnecessary psychological stuff going on, the regular psychological stuff with the military and I got extra crap on top.

So I had to keep it low key because I didn't want to go back to my hometown for nothing in the world. I had to make sure they didn't know that I am gay so I didn't get kicked out. So I had to live a double life. I married this guy. He wasn't gay though. We were just friends. So we got married so I could move out the dorm.

The One
"That's what crazy people do. When they have their heart broken they go right to god."

The relationship that Heather considers to be the most meaningful one she's had in her life was a tumultuous one, full of domestic violence and insecurities. Through it all, Heather says that she was profoundly in love with the woman but that they simply could not overcome their problems. When that relationship ended, she was broken and despondent. She was ready to turn away from the lifestyle that she believed was the cause of so much heartache and return to god.

When I was talking to her, she was all into church and stuff and she was dating this dude who was into church, too. So, she was celibate. I knew, "Oh! She ain't having sex." It was going be easy for me to come in and do something and have her change her mind. But I said, "If this relationship is going to interfere with your relationship with god, let me know and I'll back off." I respected this god shit so much that I was going to let this girl go because I didn't want to step on god's toes or some dumb shit. But my cousin told me that she liked me. That's how I called her. Now I admit, I had a girlfriend already in California, but she wasn't my ideal girl. I liked her but I loved this other girl at home. I mean I was really in love. So, I went back home and got with her. Even though people didn't like gay folks, they'd say, "Oh, y'all so beautiful as a couple." They loved us as a couple! And I loved it, too, because I was in love with her.

But she was very abusive, physically abusive, verbally abusive. Any kind of abuse you want to think of, this girl did. I guess she had that whole narcissistic personality. She'd treat me like crap but everybody else thought she was so great. It was like, "Aye! Look at these bruises! This girl ain't that great." But I didn't want to leave her because I didn't think I was ever going to get a girl that compared to her. And I must admit, to this day I haven't met a girl that I felt that way about, which kind of sucks.

During this time that we were dating, I had gotten married because we had roommates in the military barracks and I wanted my girl to come out to visit me. I didn't want her to be in the room with me and some other girl. My husband and I had dated a little bit but we were just really good friends. We both wanted to move out of the dorms and have our own apartment. So, it was just an agreement between us, just a piece of paper. So, now I had my own apartment and I was trying to get old girl to move out there but she said no. We broke up several times but she was just hell bent on getting away from me. I felt like, *I want to be with you and you're doing me wrong*. But she didn't want to deal with me anymore. There was nothing I could do about it.

So I moved to New York for a little while. I was trying to find myself. I was trying to do something. I was just trying to do whatever. I was all twisted in the head. That was the most important relationship I'd had thus far. So at that point I was a broken person. I felt like I didn't have too many friends and I couldn't keep a job. I was just a wreck. I should've gone to somebody for therapy but I didn't have the money for it. I didn't realize that I could've went to the VA and got some help. I found that out later on. So from there I was just trying to find myself.

I was still married at this point and my husband said, "Hey! You can come out and live abroad with me if you like." And I was like, "Hell yeah! I don't wanna be here any damn way! Yeah, I'll come out there." So, then I went abroad for like nine months and that was a cool experience because that was the first time I ever left the country. It was alright. My husband was agnostic. He wasn't all that spiritual. Just being around that company meant that I didn't really get into god that much. I guess I backslid from god, or whatever you want to call it. I was smoking weed a whole lot and still depressed over my ex-girlfriend. But I guess that was good in a way. It was a cool experience cause that was the first time I ever really left the country besides Canada.

Since that didn't work out, I just said, "Alright! I'm not messing around with girls anymore." Once I moved back to the U.S., I became really, really, really spiritual. That's what crazy people do. When they have their hearts broken, they go right to god as opposed to going to a psychologist or people who would talk sense to them. Instead, they go to god because that's all you hear about. But I really read the Bible and became even more crazy.

A Second Marriage
"He was agnostic. . . . That was the reason I feel we even came together in the first place."

As part of her attempt to learn more about herself, recover from her disappointing relationships, and reconnect with god, Heather chose to give heterosexuality one more try. Her second marriage, the one she says was "kinda for real," lasted two years and was as equally disappointing as her previous relationships. As she began to fully release her supernatural beliefs and faith in god, she also became more accepting of who she was as an individual. She wanted to live an authentic life.

So I gave it one more chance. I wanted a church that was multicultural and wasn't all fire and brimstone. I didn't want to be around all black folk. I wanted something different. And as soon as I went to that church, I saw this girl and I was like, "Damn! That girl is pretty!" So, I couldn't escape it. No matter what. But I met this guy and I thought he was a handsome dude. I used to have Bible study with him and there was a little chemistry between us. So I ended up dating him even though I wanted to date the girl in church. But how could I come up to her? Eventually, I thought, *Why am I wasting my time with you? I really want to date some girl up in the church and I'm dating you.*

After that relationship ended, I started dating another dude, my second husband. We started out as friends. I guess I was lonely and he was dependable and gave me attention. He was there for me. And, too, he was agnostic from the get. That was the reason I feel we even came together in the first place. I was coming away from my faith and he wasn't pushing it. He said he didn't really know, which was good for me because the guys I did date, they were all super spiritual.

When you're young, they push on you that you need to get married and have a kid and all that shit. And then they start talking that crap about your biological clock. I was about to be thirty-three on my birthday coming up and I was kind of thinking about whether or not I was going to have a child. For a clear moment I did not want to have a kid. I didn't want to have any children because I didn't have the money or the career

I wanted to have in life and I just couldn't trust people. Because I am studying psychology and seeing how people abuse children and the stuff that goes down with them, I was just paranoid about my baby. So I was like, *The best way to protect my child is to not have one.* That was my logical thinking and it worked out pretty well.

But now that I do have my son, I opted to not go back to work except on the weekends so I can give him that parent-child undivided attention for the most part. I wanted him to be able to know that his mom loves him and that he can have love himself. You don't have to go out looking for outside love like I did. I didn't have the self-esteem or love I should have had. That wasn't given to me as a child. I'll be damned if he has to go through that type of shit unless somebody kills my ass.

As far as separating from my husband, it's because he is not really allowing me to be the person I want to be. I guess he wants a traditional marriage. I don't know. I don't think a traditional marriage is for me. But when I was with him, I was going through this depression. And I figured being atheist now and not believing in a hell and not having accountability to some god that's telling me I can't do this or can't do that, it made me feel like I didn't have to be in the relationship. I don't have to suffer. I'm just hurting myself when it boils down to it. Being with him wouldn't be beneficial for my son if mommy is depressed. That's going to affect him as well. I don't want him to be unhappy, number one, or have this image of something that wasn't true. I want him to have a truthful image. So that was the thing behind that.

It would have been cool if my husband had said, "Heather, you can do what you want to do or you can have another person in the relationship." But he wanted to be all secret. "You can talk to somebody but it has to be secret." I'm like, "I'm sick of secrets!" Secrets get on my damn nerves.

Leaving Religion
"Hey! Have y'all read this part of the Bible?"

Studying psychology at a religious university is what cemented Heather's doubts about god. She chose a religious school out of a desire to feel closer to god, but the more she learned the more she could not ignore the biblical concepts that were in direct opposition to her personal values and sense of morality.

I started studying psychology in 2007 and I was going to Liberty University online because I wanted to make sure that I stayed away from The World and wasn't distracted by it. I was so brainwashed by the god concept. And with my bad experience with women, I wanted to have some happiness. And it was all working out pretty well.

What happened was that I had this one assignment and it was called "Do we really need the Bible when we have the Universal Declaration of Human Rights?" So, that made me look more into the Bible. When I saw that Jesus was cool with slavery, that was mind-blowing to me. I had already had reasons why I didn't like god and why it was hard for me to take all this stuff in but when I came across that, I said, "Why do we listen to the Bible?" It's really crappy because I saw that Jesus was cool with slavery.

I saw more and more stuff about how he was against women. I told some of my black friends from church. I was like, "Hey! Have y'all read this part of the Bible?" See, I'm thinking that nobody had read this part. You know. Maybe that's what was going on but they were so ready and willing to justify it. They said, "Well, you're a slave on your job." And I said, "No. I'm not a slave on my job. My boss never came out with a whip and start beating me because I didn't do what he said do. I mean, he might mess with my money but he don't have the right to whip me." And that was really an eye-opening experience for me. That happened around my thirtieth birthday. After that, I made it my mission to know more about this whole god thing. And that was getting me further and further away from god and it was also getting me further away from my church friends.

It was funny, too, because here I was going to this Christian college but they can't give us Christian psychology books. They have to give us the psychology books that everybody else reads. I remember that they had a disclaimer that was something like, "These books are only for class but you still have to keep your faith in god" and all this other kind of shit. So, it's like they're still trying to mess with you. For me, it wasn't working but in my classes, people were still buying it. At that time, I didn't know anybody who was an atheist. It was just me.

On Facebook, I still had friends from my hometown and friends from church. So, when I started putting these questions up and I started saying, "Hey! What about this? What about that?" everybody was like, "Girl, you going off the deep end. There's no contradiction in the Bible." But I said, "Yes there is! I'm trying to show you right here! There is a contradiction!" And they said things like, "Well, I don't know where you getting your information from." It was like I was talking to a brick wall.

It was a gradual process for me, leaving religion. When I did that paper and I found out that Jesus was cool with slavery, that hurt the most because our ancestors in America were slaves. To me, that was a big slap in my face. It was like, "Damn Jesus! You coulda stopped slavery! And right now, with black people being the bottom of the totem pole in America, you did nothing. You just said, 'I'm glad y'all believe in me. I'm glad y'all have faith in me. And matter of fact, treat your masters well.'" So, that was the turning point right there. The fact that he could have stopped me from being gay after I had been begging for years, I just kind of let that go. I thought maybe it was something inside of myself that I couldn't be straight. But to see that he had it written that he was cool with slavery! Naw! I couldn't fuck with that. But I still felt like there was some type of god.

So, I talked to my friend and she suggested something to me but she did not realize what she was doing at the time. See, I always had this mistrust of America. Being in the military and being from a poor city, I always felt like America was doing something shady. So I said, "You know what? Maybe I should go look up some religions from Africa, some of the religions that were stolen from us. Maybe that's where my happiness will be." She said, "You want to look up some African religions? Girl! Most of them are atheists." I said, "Huh? Is that right?" I don't know if she knew if that was true or not but it's almost as if, when she said it, everything became crystal clear. I was like, "You know what? Why am I messing around with some damn god? More or less, I ain't got a god cause he sure ain't there when I call on him." When I was giving tithes and offerings, the promises I was supposed to get I didn't get. With all that stuff I wasn't getting, I said, "Why am I wasting my time?" I feel like I wasted so many years submitting to some god when I could have been doing whatever the hell I wanted to do.

Fitting In
"I was expecting a backlash. And I didn't really care as much."

Heather had a few bumps in the road trying to transition socially from belief to nonbelief. She expected that her experiences from coming out as a lesbian would prepare her for what might happen when coming out as an atheist. However, she was still surprised at the extent to which the black community disdains atheism, even more than homosexuality. As with many black nonbelievers, Facebook was her only connection to like-minded black people.

An atheist. Yeah. That was much worse than me being gay. It was because people were afraid I'm going to go to hell. And there's some stuff in 2 Corinthians that basically says, "Hey, you're not supposed to be talking to people who don't believe like you believe." So, it was a scary thing to them because they thought, *Well, if she's really worshiping the devil now then I can't really be associated with that.* The thing about it is that it didn't bother me a whole lot because, like I told you, since I was eighteen I had been out the closet for homosexuality. So, I was expecting a backlash. And I didn't really care as much. I mean, it bothered me a little bit with my aunt and recently I saw that my cousin isn't my Facebook friend anymore. That kind of bothered me for a minute but now I'm like, "Yeah. Whatever."

So, the first people I looked to were the atheist groups. I typed it in and they were predominately white. I felt like I couldn't really get with their issues or whatever they had going on. I didn't have a really good vibe with them. But then I typed in "black atheists" and some shit came up! And I was like, "Oh, shit!" There was the Black Atheist Alliance and that's when I started seeing more black folks.

Facebook has really been my saving grace, as far as the whole atheist movement, because everywhere you go, people are talking about god this and god that and it's just unheard of for a black woman to not to believe in god. So, even though I definitely do not have all the facts, I guess I'm like them. They feel like Jesus is in their hearts, and I feel like god is not here in my heart. My heart is telling me that there is no god. I've been in strange relationships. I have been distraught. I have been unhappy trying to be something I am not, and if I have to go through what I'm going through now to get to my happiness, then so what. I don't care because I feel like this, *If you don't want to be cool with me, I don't want to be cool with you.*

Problems with the Church
"We're holding on to superstitions still."

Heather's advice to the black community is to learn something new. She believes that many black women will not even consider new information about the Bible out of fear—fear of the possibility of increased doubt. Even still, she is hopeful that as people see more happy, healthy black atheists, they will open their minds.

You know what? I have a theory about those folks who won't talk to atheists. With those folks, they feel like they are already so close to not following god that you'll be a big influence on them to let go of god as well. I think soon things will get to the point where there is more of an atheist nation because of the Internet where you can cross-reference and access stuff that's in the Bible. You can see the destruction of what religion has done in some places and you can see the hypocrisy of things. I think that, as people see more of us who are atheists and that good things actually happen in our lives, they will realize, "Man! There probably is a hope."

I think that the generation before us and even our generation, they are the ones who keep hating, thinking they got some wisdom or something. Yeah, they may have some wisdom, how to cook or whatever. But as far as the god thing, I don't think they have the wisdom on that. I think the only people who might have some wisdom on that are the ones who've lived a long time and who can say, "You know what? There might not be a god." Even Mother Teresa was saying that she had her doubts. She wrote that she had some doubts and that she may have wasted her life doing this.

The problem is that we don't learn anything new. We're holding on to superstitions still. They're trying to get better with the homophobic thing but it's still there, especially in black society. They still got the homophobic thing going on and that's uncool for folks like me. They tell you that you need to read your Bible, but I don't think that people actually do it. It's sad because they know people aren't going to read that whole big prehistoric book. They also need to talk about the slavery part. But really, we just need to get rid of the Black Church. That's what I say.

12

STEPHANIE'S STORY

Childhood Experiences
"I would literally sit in church and roll my eyes the whole time."

Stephanie is a twenty-four year old Haitian-born woman who moved to the United States when she was seven years old. Even though her mother was not intensely involved in church, Stephanie grew up attending a Baptist church on a regular basis. However, she was not prepared for what she experienced when she moved in with her uncle and his family. While she remembers her early exposure to religion as a relatively harmless experience, she recalls being overwhelmed by the intensity of her uncle's religious practices in her teenage years. And in that situation, her curious mind was already starting to question.

I was born in Haiti and grew up Baptist. When we moved here, we did the whole church thing but, to us, Christianity was just about going to church on Sunday. My mother was not your old type of Christian. She wasn't in church Monday through Friday. So, it was easier for me because I just went to church on Sundays.

What happened was that, during my teenage years, I started not getting along with my mother and I moved out and started living with my uncle's family. They are really into the church. They went to church on Monday, Wednesday, Friday, Saturday, and Sunday. I thought, *Oh my god!* It was crazy. I was in church every day and everything that happened in the house was "*god, god, and god.*" So I started going more. I joined the choir. I was an usher. I also joined different groups that the church had. But, in the back of my mind I thought, *I don't really believe this crap, I don't believe it.* It never made any sense to me. I had questions and every time I asked them, I never got an answer that was sufficient. I never got an answer that made any sense.

After a while, I gave up and said, "I can't do this crap anymore! I can't keep going to church." I felt really unhappy. I can't even explain it. I became so depressed and it was a struggle for me because I believed I was atheist but I did not want to admit it. So, I kept going to church, but everything the preacher was talking about was so against what I stood for that I became really depressed. I couldn't really make friends in the church because I would literally sit in church and roll my eyes the whole time. So I ended up leaving and going back to live with my mom. It was like a breath of fresh air because, with my mom, I didn't have to go to church.

College and the Beginning of Atheism
"I'm not going to church anymore; I don't want to hear that B.S."

As with many nonbelievers, Stephanie's decision to leave religion behind was primarily the result of studying Christianity more closely than she had in the past.

Freshman year in college I came back and I picked it right up again. I started going to church because I was fighting the fact that I knew I was atheist. I thought, *Wait. If I'm not Christian, if I'm not Baptist, how am I going to live? Am I going to be a sinner? I don't want to go to hell!* So, I went to church freshman year. Nobody forced me to go. I just thought it was the Christian thing to do. It wasn't until I met this guy who I was with for five years and who was very open-minded that I could have these conversations. He wasn't an atheist and he didn't fully agree with my atheism but he was willing to really sit down with me and help me to see things differently. A lot of the questions that I had, he answered them.

So, I picked up the Bible and I started reading it on my own. My sophomore year is when I said, "That's it! I'm not going to church anymore; I don't want to hear that B.S. I'm an atheist and that's it!" I don't think I even went further than Genesis. It was contradictory; you would read one thing in this chapter and then read another thing in that chapter. I had these questions that nothing you could say would make sense. It just didn't make any sense. One of the questions I had was about the idea that it was just Adam and Eve in the beginning and they laid together and made Cain and Abel. Then I thought, *Who did Cain and Abel lay with?* I remember that one time the answer I got was, "Well back in the day, incest was okay, it wasn't until. . ." I just thought, *Wait a minute, you're teaching me that god never changes and that god makes no mistakes but now you're basically telling me that back in the day incest was okay, even though now it's not okay.* That's when I said, "I'm over it! I don't want to hear this anymore." And that was it for me.

Questions
"Don't get it twisted. Don't mistake the privileges that you have living here as god's work."

The harder Stephanie tried to find some truth, the more she doubted. She even went through the common phase of blaming the inconsistency, hypocrisy, and confusion found in Christianity on the fallibility of humans. She tried to hold on to the belief that god was still god and he was good, but as the questions piled up, the explanations crumbled.

I had this journal and I had all these questions that I would write down. I would go around and just have random discussions with anybody that I could find. Anyone that was willing to talk to me or answer my questions, whether it was online with an atheist group or whether they were Christian or whatever. I just wanted to hear the different interpretations. When I got answers from people who were Christians, they never made sense to me. I always used to wonder, *Why do we even need a New Testament? Why does Jesus even have to die on a cross for our sins?* To me, it simply meant that god made a mistake and that he knew that he would send someone down here to correct that mistake. Nobody could really give me a clear answer to that.

The second question was, *If god knows everything that was going to happen, why did he allow Eve to eat the fruit?* He knew what was going to happen. What made it easier for me to stay in church, though, was that I just said to myself, "Okay, well maybe everyone else has the wrong god. This is the wrong god. Or the Bible was written by men and men got it all twisted up. Maybe god is not like this. Maybe there is a god but he is not like this at all."

Another question was about why he allowed bad things to happen? I used to hate when people would say, "I'm blessed and highly favored." I'm thinking, *Okay, what about the kids in the third world countries that are starving and who are dying every day of starvation? Did god just turn his back on them? Are they not blessed and highly favored?* I didn't get that. My life has been great and it had nothing to do with me praying, nothing with to do with god favoring me more. It's because I had more opportunity. I was sick and tired of people, especially in the Western world, saying everything was because of god. That just pissed me off! I come from Haiti and I am really surprised at how we live this American life. Everything here is god, god, god. Don't get it twisted. Don't mistake the privileges that you have living here as god's work.

Coming Out
"There is just something in us that allowed us to be free and open."

Stephanie says that coming out of the closet as an atheist was not as big of an ordeal for her as it is for many other black women. However, she says that she still struggles with some of the psychological residue from years of indoctrination.

Now as far as coming out to my family members, that was not hard. I'm a don't-give-a-fuck kind of person. I remember my mother and my grandmother had the conversation once about a verse and they started talking about god. I just said that I didn't agree and they all looked at me with shock. I told them exactly how I felt. My grandma said, "Wait. Let me ask you a question. Are you a Christian?" I said, "Well, I'm glad that you asked because, actually, I'm not." My grandma said that she would pray for me. We got into another conversation about another chapter in the Bible. I told her exactly how I felt about it and she said, "Okay, I understand you." My mother is like that too. She's the kind of person who would say, "Okay, well live your life as long as you are a good person." I don't believe I'm a bad person. I try to make the best choices for myself as well as the people that are around me. I would therefore hope that my family will judge me by that and not by my lack of religious belief.

I understand people who are religious because I know it is a hard thing to give up. I will admit that it's all still new to me. Even now sometimes I kind of revert back a little to some Christian thoughts. Sometimes, there are certain things that happen in my life when I don't know what else to do. I feel that I should just jump right back in. Atheists have to understand that about believers. It's not so much that we atheists are smarter or better. There is just something in us that allowed us to be free and open. But for the majority of people, not so much. It's not going to happen.

Emotional and Psychological Impact
"Pretty much everything was a sin and everything would lead to you going to hell."

Stephanie's attempts to figure out the truth and make a real effort to be a good Christian created a number of emotional and psychological traumas for her.

Well, okay, let's go to the topic of hell first. As a child, that is pretty much the first thing you know of. That's the way your parents brainwash you into accepting god. If you don't except this god, you're going to go to hell. That alone is extremely damaging for a child's psyche. I always had that fear. I used to fear going to hell so bad that I used to dream about it. I would stay in my room, pray and read the Bible but still I would dream that I went to hell. I remember I had three episodes where I had three different dreams that I did not make it into heaven. All those times, I would wake up from my sleep and say, "Oh my God! Oh my God!

I did something wrong." I can't even describe it. I don't know if other people go through that but to worry about something so bad that you are dreaming about it, that's very damaging.

In my aunt's and uncle's house, everything was a sin. I love dancing but as soon as I moved into that home, I could not dance anymore because apparently that was a sin. This was hard-core religious. Wearing pants was a sin. A child could not have an opinion. You are just supposed to do and react the way they want you to react and there were beatings because the Bible says so. Pretty much everything was a sin and everything could lead you to hell. They tried to force me to get baptized. There was the idea that, if I didn't get baptized and I died, I would go to hell, even if I had accepted God or Christ as my personal savior. So that was a fear I had. I opted to not get baptized but I thought, *I'm going to hell.*

In the church. . . oh god! The hypocrites! I mean, it was just so bad. We came to church one day and found out that one of the ladies from church was pregnant by the pastor. That was a big scandal. I tried to refrain from all types of sins because I believed that they were going to send me to hell, but to come to church and see people that you looked up to doing all this crap or to read the Bible and for the Bible to tell you one thing and then for the members of your church to do another thing, it was really confusing, to say the least.

I also got messages that sometimes it wasn't your sin but your parent's sins that caused problems. All that did for me was make me say, "God is an evil-ass jerk! Why would you make me pay for what my parents did? I'm an innocent child." I remember there was a child born with fetal alcohol syndrome and the preacher said that the child deserved it because the parents were bad. Yes. The mother was drinking through her pregnancy and that's a horrible thing to do but they almost made it seem like they were glad it happened because it showed that it's okay for the sins of your parents to come down to you. I would wonder what sins my mom and dad committed. Everything that happened to me would make me think, *Oh my God, I think my mom and dad committed sin.* It's a vicious, evil cycle. It was horrible!

Money

"It's not about religion, a higher being, morals or values—it's just about money."

The financial conflict that is present in the lives of many black church members recently reared its head in Stephanie's family. The money problem in the church raises huge questions for her about what the Black Church is doing with the money.

What I realized was that, in the end, it was all about money. Take single motherhood for example. You know the Bible speaks against that but the preachers would never ever bring that up because they knew that the church was made up of about 70 to 80 percent women and a good half of them were single mothers. It was their money that was coming into the church. He would not preach about that because he knew he would lose a great deal of his congregation. He would not talk about the men who walked out of their kids' lives because he was afraid of stepping on people's toes. It's not about religion, a higher being, morals or values—it's just about money in that collection plate every Sunday. Money makes the world go around.

Just take my mom as an example. Every pay she gets, she gives her ten percent. When I started working, I told her that there were certain bills that she had that I would take care of. A couple of weeks ago, I called her and she said, "Oh Steph, don't forget to pay my phone bill." She told me that her husband gave her some money for the phone bill, but, instead of paying the phone bill, she gave it to the church. My mom's cell phone comes to about a hundred and something dollars, but she gives a hundred and something dollars to the church. So I told her, "You'll have to come up with that money to pay for your cell phone." I feel bad for saying that to her because I have the money and could easily pay it, but I felt I had to make her learn a lesson. Her belief is that, when she's really in a jam, the church is going to be there. She would say, "You never know. Something might happen and they're going to be there." I said, "Mom I've never seen it happen!"

I went to this church for years and people would lose their homes, jobs, and family but the church never came through to help. It was actually the members in the church who, when someone was in a jam, would make a collection among themselves and give it to that other member. But I never saw a church do it. So it's extremely hard financially on the black community. Let's be for real! The black community, as far as finances, is on the lowest on the totem pole. We have to take what money we have and give it to the church but nothing is happening. The churches are not helping the community. Have you ever seen these massive churches in these horrible communities? They're not opening community centers. They're not really putting on anything to keep the kids out of the street. They're not doing anything. Teenage pregnancies are still on the rise in these communities. Obesity, hypertension, all these medical issues that are the black community as a whole and no one is addressing the fact that all the money is going to the church. What are they doing with that money?

Relationships and Atheism
"I would pray for days and ask for forgiveness, but it was so good that I went back and I did it again."

While Stephanie has been lucky enough to avoid romantic relationship problems as an adult atheist, as a teenager she ran into the usual bump in the psychological road—sex outside of marriage.

Relationship-wise, I'll be honest with you. I've only met two atheist men in my whole entire life. The first time that I met a man who was an atheist, I was not ready to admit that I, myself, was an atheist, so I pushed him away. When he told me that he was an atheist, I thought, *Oh my God! How could you?* This was my freshman year at college. Part of me admired him and the other part of me was just scared shitless because I had never met someone who was an atheist before. So, that relationship never had a chance to flourish. Then, about a year ago, I met another guy that was an atheist and it was like a breath of fresh air. The relationship was amazing, amazing, amazing but it still didn't work out. It takes more than being an atheist to make the relationship work.

Other than that, everyone I've dated has always had some kind of religion. Whether it was Catholic, Baptist, whatever it was, they were Christian. I never had a big issue. Right from the get-go I let them know: "Look, I don't believe this. I don't care what you believe. I don't want to hear about it." And that was that. I find that women tend to be more religious than men. So, men are a little more open-minded to the idea. Some men say, "No! I want a god-fearing woman!" They just want to know that the woman is going to be a traditional woman as the Bible describes. But for the most part, most men I meet don't really care.

In high school, I was a little sinner! When I had sex, I admit, I had a lot of guilt. *Oh my god, I just had sex out of wedlock and I am going to hell!* I would pray for days and ask for forgiveness, but it was so good that I went back and I did it again. So yes, I went through that. Because there was no way to go back, that bothered me for a while. That's the part that did not go away until I came to terms with my atheism.

Problem with the Black Church
"Education will lead you to so many possibilities."

As a highly educated black woman, Stephanie believes wholeheartedly in the value of a quality education and the important role the community plays in ensuring the success of its youth. The problem, in her opinion, is that the Black Church does not honor that role often enough.

The biggest problem in the Black Church is the lack of education. To me, education will lead you to so many possibilities and opportunities. The lack of education only leads to poor health. The lack of education only leads to not really taking care of our community, point blank! We are so quick to condemn everyone. But you know what I find really funny, none of this is just the "Black Church." It's any church. The people that really need help, they don't help them because they condemn them. I will give you an example. Say you have a child in the church who has all these opportunities like me. They will take the child and they will bring him in front of the church in front of the congregation and they'll say, "Look at what God has done!" Then the kid that never had this opportunity or who ended up doing bad things or the girl that got pregnant at the age of thirteen or the one who got an STD or something horrible happened, they never bring that kid in front of the church and say, "Well, look what we did. We turned our backs on her." They are going to say, "Look what the devil did." I'm thinking, *Wait, all you had to do was open your arms to this child. I am sure they would have come out okay.*

13

ON COGNITIVE DISTORTIONS

"And Thou Shalt Think an Evil Thought"
—Ezekial 38:10

In the mental health field, we talk about cognitive distortions being a culprit behind emotional turmoil. Simply put, a cognitive distortion is when a person's thoughts or opinions are formed without consideration of the facts or without evidence. There are several types of cognitive distortions with which a person could struggle, and religious thinking requires a person to employ them all.

Black-and-White Thinking

Black-and-white thinking could also be thought of as all-or-nothing thinking. Most Christian denominations hate theories like "situational ethics," because they believe such concepts to be a ticket for people to do anything they want. You often hear people of this mind-set say things like, "What's right is right and what's wrong is wrong" or "Sin is sin." Because of this particular thinking error, black-and-white thinkers are prone to believe that their religious orientation is the only right one. In their minds, they hold the key to unlocking god's blessings in life and the afterlife. This creates the atmosphere of intolerance that is so prevalent in our society today. Black women have not been able to escape the harm of this cognitive distortion.

This type of thinking sets up a person for disappointment by creating unrealistic expectations for themselves and others. For example, black women sometimes hold themselves back from progress. They may have limited themselves in their careers or in relationships because of their religious beliefs. I have known black women who have turned down jobs, promotions, and raises because accepting them might interfere with their ability to attend church on a regular basis. They would say that you could know that the job truly is from god by whether or not it would prevent them from going to church. The socioeconomic and psychological implications of those kinds of beliefs are endless.

I have also seen this sort of thinking interfere with relationships. Black women often say that they only want a boyfriend or husband who is into church and they therefore pass on potentially good partners. And we all probably know gay people who are estranged from families because of their sexual orientation. These are more examples of black-and-white thinking at work that create a painful kind of conditional love.

Overgeneralization

Overgeneralization is the cognitive distortion in which a person comes to a general conclusion based on a single incident or piece of evidence. If something happens once, it will happen again. This is the source of destructive forces like stereotypes. If one person is a certain way, all people who have similarities to that person are that same way. Religious people often perpetuate hateful overgeneralizations and stereotypes about groups of people with whom they disagree.

The problem black women face is that black churches spread all kinds of overgeneralizations and they indoctrinate their members with beliefs about things for which there is little or no evidence. Of course, the primary source of poor evidence is the Bible. Because Ruth got a good husband by being submissive, all women should behave as Ruth did. Because Ananias and Sapphira dropped dead for not giving all their money to god, all people will be cursed who do not give enough to the church (Acts 5:1–11). Because Jonah was swallowed by a fish for his disobedience, all disobedient people will be harshly punished (Jonah 1). What's worse is that the punishment is usually totally unrelated to the sin. Black churches and ministers also lean heavily on anecdotal evidence to support their claims. Because one woman had a failed relationship with a person who was not saved, all "unequally yoked" relationships are doomed to fail (2 Corinthians 6:14–17).

Another way to think about overgeneralizations is in relation to coincidences and confirmation bias. Christians often see miraculous events in everyday coincidences. If a person uses bill money to pay tithes and then an unexpected and unrelated refund shows up in the mail, they overgeneralize the incident. The event reinforces their conviction that giving their last dime to the church is a good thing. What they do not consider, however, is all the times they gave their last dime with no windfall or they had to borrow money to pay their heating bill. Even negative coincidences are seen as signs or proof of something. If a woman gets into a car accident on the way to church, it might be seen as the devil trying to stop her from getting a blessing.

Black women struggle with overgeneralizations and stereotypes everyday, but they do not seem to overcome them on any widespread or consistent basis. They accept the overgeneralizations the church imposes on them socially, financially, and emotionally. They settle for less based on unreliable evidence and information because of the trust they place in the ministers and institutions that push these agendas. They do not work to develop their own critical thinking skills when it comes to church and instead surrender their will and power to others.

Focusing on the Negative

This form of cognitive distortion is exactly what it sounds like—the individual is only willing or able to dwell on negative things. If something good happens, they always find a negative angle from which to view it.

We all know people like that and we dread being around them. They are usually grumpy, irritable, or easily angered. These people can find all kinds of reasons to be unhappy, and when they are happy, it is usually short-lived. The Black Church can be a very negative institution. And because of its authority in the black community, its negativism spreads quickly. For example, the church is consumed by the need to point out sin and to remind people that they could end up in hell. The women who dole out these reminders usually think they are being helpful and showing love when they implore their family members to give up their sinful lifestyles and return to god.

Furthermore, the messages of one's innately sinful nature and the constant threat of hell cause black women to internalize these messages and create their own neuroses. Because of their need to be strong for others, black women do not often admit their worries about themselves. Bombarded with messages of sin and death and hell and rarely fed genuinely uplifting messages (those that do not come with conditions and restrictions), black women are led to focus on the negatives inside of themselves and in their families without even realizing they are doing it, because those are the thoughts the church has seared into their brains.

Discounting the Positive

Unlike focusing on the negative, with discounting the positive, the sufferer can see and recognize something good but insists that her or someone else's accomplishments and positive qualities do not count. At best, a woman will simply ignore good qualities and accomplishments. At worst, she will openly disparage herself or others. You can see this particular cognitive distortion in play at almost any testimonial service. A testimonial service is a portion of a church service during which members are encouraged to stand in front of the entire congregation and share the good things that god has been doing for them. A natural part of praising god is downplaying the self. It is not unusual for people to start their testimonies with phrases like "I'm just a sinner" and verses of "Amazing Grace." Because all things that are good supposedly flow from god—"Every good and perfect gift is from above and cometh down from the father" (James 1:17)—black women are not allowed to believe that they have, in any way, contributed to the good things in their lives.

If a woman is smart, the Holy Spirit told her the answers. If she makes good money, it is a result of god's blessing from faithfully paying her tithes. If she has a happy marriage and family, it is because she is submissive to her husband. In other words, her intelligence is not a result of genetics or hard studying. Her good job is not the result of her education, strong work ethic, or networking skills. Her happy home is not the result of her commitment, communication skills, or parenting skills. Nothing good in her life has anything to do with who she is as a person but everything to do with god.

She must not forget to constantly give god all credit and praise, lest her pride cause god to take her blessings away. Black women already have a tough lot in life and unfortunate standing in society, battling the twin "-isms" of sexism and racism. The last thing they need is another voice telling them that they are not worth much on their own. These sorts of messages become entrenched in a woman's heart and mind, especially after generations of grandmothers, aunts, mothers, and cousins spread the same idea. No matter how successful and self-confident she may appear to be, a god-fearing woman's life is likely to be littered with periods of defeat and depression. So when times get tough, her natural inclination will be to praise god and, by necessity, disparage herself and discount her positives.

Jumping to Conclusions

Jumping to conclusions is a thinking error that involves drawing conclusions that are not warranted by acts. There are two types of thinking errors that involve jumping to conclusions: mind reading—assuming that people are reacting negatively to you; and fortune-telling—predicting that things will turn out badly. It is not hard to see how these cognitive distortions might surface frequently among churchgoers. Because the Black Church is composed of conservative, biblical literalists, these types of cognitive distortions are easily manifested in the concepts such as prophesying and discerning of spirits. They take verses such as Acts 2:17

as literal fact: "You sons and daughters shall prophesy, and your young men shall see visions, and your old men shall dream dreams."

Mind Reading

Since the Christian god is by nature a cognitively distorted mind reader, it should come as no surprise that many of his so-called prophets and evangelists believe that they, too, can read minds with guidance from the Master Mind Reader. As a result, black women become hypervigilant about their thoughts because of the belief that the thoughts themselves could potentially be sinful. In Matthew 5:28 Jesus says, "But I say unto you, that whosoever looketh on a woman to lust after her hath committed adultery with her already in his heart." So, the black woman is in a constant state of fear that god is judging her and she is, therefore, in a perpetual state of monitoring her thoughts. And that becomes exhausting.

Furthermore, since religion is, in and of itself, such a divisive system, many believers think that they are somehow the minority in a sea of sinful infidels. They assume that they know more about nonbelievers than the nonbelievers know about themselves because they, the faithful, have The Truth in the word of god. Mind reading, assuming that you know what others are thinking, and believing that you are a perpetual victim in society do not foster openness to new ideas—they create a deeper sense of isolation.

Fortune-Telling

Fortune-telling involves predicting that things will turn out badly. Sex is a favorite topic for prophets. Sex before marriage is presented by the church as being the scariest, most dangerous act possible. Churchgoers often predict the worst possible consequences for sex. Brokenheartedness. Disease. Death. Eternal Damnation. Before marriage, there is hardly anything positive to say about sex or the prospects of those who engage in it. Even after marriage, things turn out badly for people who talk dirty, watch pornography, or use toys. Those lascivious actions can only lead to increased lustiness, adultery, and eventually eternal damnation.

Another issue about which the church likes to make negative

predictions is regarding tithing and offering. Although the "prosperity gospel" is presumably focused on the benefits of giving to god, in reality it highlights the consequences of holding back. For example, prosperity gospel preachers often refer to Deuteronomy 28, an entire book devoted to highlighting the blessings and curses of god, in their sermons. The problem is that only 14 of the 68 verses in that chapter are dedicated to highlighting the blessings of god, while the remaining 54 verses focus on the potential curses that could result from disobeying god.

Christianity, in general, depends on fortune-telling. In order to sell the concept of an everlasting life, Christianity has to have a carrot to dangle. As Norm Allen says, "Fundamentalist Christians have been playing silly mind games with themselves and terrorizing their fellow human beings by making gloomy predictions for two thousand years."[1] Fortune-telling and focusing on the negative go hand in hand because, and this is especially true of the Bible, it seems that life's negatives are much more worthy of our attention than the positives.

Minimization and Magnification

Minimization and magnification essentially involve shrinking the significance of an event or blowing it out of proportion in one of two ways: minimizing your or others' mistakes, or magnifying your or others' mistakes.

Minimization

Christianity posits the idea that, if you ask anything in Jesus' name, you can be forgiven. So, while we make many mistakes, we can simply ask for forgiveness and reasonably expect others to easily move past those transgressions as well. When it comes to forgiveness, black women get a lot of conflicting responses, especially when they think they should be forgiven but their community does not forgive them. Black women who minimize their own mistakes are likely to become very frustrated and hurt when people do not immediately offer forgiveness. Indeed, minimizing one's own mistakes can create a lot of resentment toward those who do not agree that a particular transgression should be so easily forgiven and quickly forgotten. As part of the inherently judgmental nature of the Black Church, a woman may ironically be simultaneously magnifying someone else's sins while minimizing her own.

When you think of what it means to minimize other people's mistakes, the concept of enabling comes to mind. Minimizing the mistakes of others often requires the person to ignore events or actions that can be very egregious in nature. A prime example that we see in the news almost every day involves the seemingly endless cases of sexual abuse perpetrated by pastors and priests. Often the most shocking details are that there were other leaders or individuals close to the accused who knew of the transgressions and did nothing about them. In many cases, after all of the details have come out—even after a confession—there are church members who will stand by the person in the name of godly love and forgiveness and refuse to condemn the person's actions.

Magnification

Magnifying one's own mistakes is problematic for obvious reasons. First of all, it engenders much guilt, anxiety, and depression. When black women hyperfocus on their own mistakes, they may find themselves fasting, attending prayer meetings and Bible studies three or four days a week, or constantly praying for forgiveness. Most likely the supposed sins they have committed are completely normal and to be expected. Events as major as premarital sex to instances as minor as overeating have all been known to lead to excessive amounts of repentant activities such as fasting, confession, and prayer. And because some of these "sins" are completely normal human behaviors, the woman who goes through this process will find her guilt and frustration growing because she will likely commit the same "sins" over and over.

Magnifying others' mistakes also occurs quite frequently. It goes hand in hand with many of the other distortions, because it invariably leads to a highly judgmental perspective on life. For example, black women may find themselves angry and frustrated as a result of seeing other women make what they believe are mistakes, or they may find themselves victims of another person's magnifying wrath. Obviously, this can lead to any number of emotional and social problems such as isolation, sadness, and frustration, as these women continue to try so hard to do what they can to please god.

Emotional Reasoning

Emotional reasoning is the cognitive distortion of making assumptions, judgments, and decisions based on emotions. A person with this thinking error may find herself saying, "I feel like a failure; therefore, I must be a failure." "I feel like an idiot; therefore, I am." And on and on. Emotional reasoners also find themselves validating their beliefs based on emotions. For example, the church service in which she shouted and felt the glory of god must be proof that god is going to bless her. But when she does not get blessed, she is hurt. She says, "This blessing didn't happen. I must have done something wrong and that caused me to miss my blessing. I must be a sinner." Since emotions are the powerhouse that fuel behavior, emotional reasoning can bind a woman to the church in a way that makes it most difficult to free herself.

"Should" Statements

"Should" statements involve criticizing oneself or others with "shoulds," "shouldn'ts," "musts," "oughts," and "have tos." Churchgoers have likely heard statements such as:

- "A woman of god SHOULD be at church every time the doors open."
- "A virtuous woman SHOULDN'T use profanity."
- "A faithful woman MUST obey her husband."
- "A Christian woman OUGHT to abstain from premarital sex."
- "In order to be happy and successful, godly women HAVE TO have so much faith that they only speak the things they want."

Black women face a constant barrage of religious "should" statements that control and oppress every aspect of their lives. Women may also find themselves judging others based on the "should" statements of their church. This, of course, only breeds strife and fighting among the very women who should be supporting each other. As Darrel Ray reminds, "The great psychotherapist Dr. Albert Ellis called this the 'tyranny of the should.' He often said in his workshops, 'Shouldhood leads to shithood. Don't should on yourself, and don't should on others—it stinks.'"[2] In some denominations, there are proscriptions that dictate how you can style your hair and how much jewelry you can wear. In black churches, black women are especially susceptible to messages about how they should be submissive wives and how submissive wives must behave. The list of "should" statements regarding sex, church attendance, finances, relationships, and all areas of a person's life is endless. The implications of being unable to meet the requirements of each "should" statement are immediately clear. It only serves to deepen a woman's depression and insecurity when she finds that she cannot fully measure up to the church's expectations.

Name-Calling

Name-calling is the concept that a person generalizes one or two qualities or events into negative global judgments. Instead of saying, "I made a mistake," she says, "I'm a failure." A person may also name call others. For example, instead of saying, "She's having a bad day," a name-caller might say, "She's a total bitch!" As we go through all of these cognitive distortions, we can clearly see how many of the distortions are extremely guilt inducing and result in extreme emotional distress. The church tells women that one mistake makes them a sinner in need of a lot of penance. If a black woman has premarital sex even once, she is a fornicator. If she wears a revealing dress, she is a Jezebel. If she does not pay her tithes, she's a robber (Malachi 3:8). And so on.

Blame

Blame, as a cognitive distortion, is about using blame instead of finding solutions. The Bible, Christianity, and the Black Church are built on blame and the resulting guilt. The most famous and epic example of blame is Eve's sin. Another example is that the church may hold a woman responsible for a man's temptation if she is nicely dressed. But while the church does a lot of blaming, black women are also blaming themselves. If they are having a particularly chronic problem in life, they often blame themselves for doing something wrong. If a woman cannot pay her bills, maybe it is her fault for not making a larger offering. Even more ridiculous than blaming herself or others is blame that she places on demons and the devil. Thus, if her child is having behavioral problems, it may be that she let him watch Harry Potter and he "picked up a demon." When her car breaks down, it is the devil trying to stop her from getting to the house of god. Forget the fact that it may have been a year since her car's last oil change. When she is sick, it is the devil trying to weaken her spirit as opposed to a common virus or seasonal allergies. Clearly, the blame game can get quite ridiculous in the context of religion.

We all have our own cognitive distortions with which we struggle (see appendix 3). Even the most well-adjusted and sane person will have some cognitive distortions to fight off in her day-to-day life. But certain environments and situations are perfect for the growth of insidious thinking errors. On top of the cognitive distortions caused by religion in general and its inherent denial of reality, the Black Church creates additional layers of distortions in the minds of black women due to its particular dynamics and practices. Faced with such a focus on sin and guilt, tough mores about gender roles, and longstanding methods of indoctrinating, black women fight an uphill battle to beat the effects of religiously based cognitive distortions.

14

MANDISA'S STORY

Childhood Experiences
"Christianity was never something I wanted to understand anyway."

Mandisa is a thirty-four-year old woman from New York who, in January 2011, along with Benjamin Burchall, cofounded a now-flourishing atheist group in Georgia, Black Nonbelievers of Atlanta. Because of her past experiences with religious friends and families, she feels a strong desire to help educate and liberate questioning believers and to provide the much-needed support and sense of community that many ex-believers look for after exiting the religions of their families. Mandisa avoided most of the woes of a religious upbringing because her mother was more concerned about Mandisa's cultural education than spiritual education. However, Mandisa was exposed to Christianity and other religions through the community in which she lived and her family.

First, I was born and raised in Jamaica Queens in the projects by a single parent. My father's mother is a Christian and she is extremely religious. She has had a very strong influence on that side of the family. I do see pictures where we did go to church with her as a child or before I could remember. But my mother did not raise us to be Christians. As a child, I would perform in various churches under the direction of my voice instructor. So, I was exposed to many church services.

When my mother and my father split, she got involved in the Five Percenters, you know, Nation of Gods and Earths. So, I was exposed to certain aspects of Islam as well. Also, we would go to a cultural center called the Afrikan Poetry Theatre with some Christians and some Muslims as well as people who had adopted some African culture and religions. In essence, I was raised to be a Black Nationalist. I also had a cultural teacher who I used to recite poetry under. She was very much Afrocentric and a Christian as well. I was never isolated from any religious people.

The imagine of White Jesus just never made any sense to me. It would kind of creep me out especially with me growing up learning about how slavery was imposed and forced upon Africans when they came to America. So, I would just never understand how black people could worship a white god. I tried to read the Bible as a kid, about seven or eight. I was probably like your typical Christian who would hear certain passages from the Bible but never understand it. The paradoxical nature of a loving god who's going to condemn you to hell if you don't believe in him never appealed to me at all.

I remember my mother letting me go to church with my grandmother a couple of times if I asked her. Because my mother didn't want me raised around that side of the family, I would seldom go around them. And I remember one time going to the Sunday school class and I didn't have any money to chip in. My grandmother said, "Well, you know you gotta give to the church." She would always try to put that guilt trip on you that a lot of religious people do. And almost everything out of her mouth is "praise the lord" and "the lord woke me up this morning" and "god this and god that." My cousins would always do that, too. But they were those hypocritical Christians. I felt really estranged.

Family Dynamics
"They were your typical dysfunctional family. But they hid behind their religious beliefs."

Mandisa's relationship with her father's side of the family was tenuous at best. She says that, even though her mother was not thrilled about her spending

time with that side of the family, she tried to have a relationship with them.
Over the years, she was exposed to some of the insidious concepts that are part
of the foundation of the Black Church.

My paternal grand poppy, from what I understand, wasn't really religious,
but my paternal grandmother was. Interacting with them, they say very
mean and rude things as a family. I think that a lot of these people use
their religious beliefs to cover up their shortcomings as individuals.
Religion just masks that. They were your typical dysfunctional family.
But they hid behind their religious beliefs. So, there are a lot of problems
about my paternal grandmother in her nature and her personality. For
example, I called her on her birthday last month in March and she didn't
immediately pick up the phone because she said she didn't recognize the
number. She said, "Oh, you know I don't know anyone down there."
And I'm thinking to myself, *404? That automatically means me.* I'm the
only one of the grandchildren that lives down here. It's almost like "out of
sight out of mind" thing. And of course my cousins and my other family
members, they just love this woman. She can be very nice and she has a
few shortcomings but because she praises god and Jesus, it's overlooked
by a lot of family members. I would say that in black culture, there's
definitely a lot of reverence for the matriarch of the family no matter
what. My mom's side of the family wasn't as religious as my father's side.
However, a few of my uncles are. One of my uncles is a Muslim. He lives
in Texas and he's one of their ministers.

I have another uncle who was very much into Jimmy Swaggart. He
would take us to Six Flags Great Adventures once a year and we would
have to be subjected to him listening to this Christian music. Oh god!
We rode with him in his car from New York to New Jersey to go there.
We had to listen to this Christian music, his Jimmy Swaggart tapes.
He would say, "If you don't believe in Jesus you're going to hell." And
I remember hearing pieces of that while I was trying to sleep. It was
torture! I thought it was stupid.

One time when I was fourteen, I had a debate with one of my cousins
on my father's side of the family and she was talking about the original
sin. She said that when we're born, we're all born in sin. And of course

by me not being raised in religion, I asked her how that's possible when babies are born not knowing anything. They don't know enough to know what is a sin. So, I guess in my mind that never made sense.

Did You Ever Believe? Even a Little?
"You couldn't just pull one over on me with the whole Jesus thing."

The fact that Mandisa's mother was more focused on ensuring that Mandisa had a solid awareness of social and cultural issues going on in the world contributed to Mandisa never being convinced by anyone to believe in Christianity. Although she went through a period of time when she did believe in a higher power, this belief was never tied to the sort of organized religion that her extended family was used to.

For the longest time, I would say "creator" because I never identified with a religion per se. But, being raised Afrocentric and as a Black Nationalist, a lot them believed in spirits. They believed in a higher being or a higher power, though I would never say it was a Christian god or Jesus. As a teenager, I would say, "I'm not religious; I'm spiritual," because I thought being spiritual was being one with god. As a Black Nationalist, we were learning about real children who were suffering. We were learning about apartheid in South Africa and what was happening to children. I grew up learning about what actually happened during slavery, things like lynching. So, those images stuck with me the longest time. Knowing that real people suffered had a bigger impact on me and made me more of a humanist.

Going to the cultural center was almost like a church community. I grew up having a lot of fun with other children my age and we learned a lot. But it was almost like a cult in that there was a lot of intermarrying. It was almost like wife swapping in that a lot of them had long-time families and children with some women and next thing you know they were having kids with some other women. And these women were friends. I remember my mother saying she was not going to be involved in that and she broke away from that.

I am an atheist. In fact, the first time I said I was an atheist was when I was fourteen because someone had asked me if I was an atheist and I had to ask them what that meant. They said it means that you don't believe in heaven or hell. I had to say yes. I don't believe in the devil. I don't subscribe to any of those beliefs. So, that would be correct. People saw me as that strong black teenager who didn't take any shit. You couldn't just pull one over on me with the whole Jesus thing.

Adult Life as an Atheist
"I just don't believe. I never have believed. I just don't."

Although Mandisa did not struggle with belief and unbelief the way many black women do, she still had a moment of clarity when she realized that she had begun calling herself an agnostic, as opposed to an atheist, because of the cultural implications of calling oneself an atheist.

I would say that I really, really came full circle in 2008. I never thought about it too much when I was in New York or when I moved down here to Atlanta. But when one of the first questions they ask you is, "What church do you go to?" that's when I really came to the realization. Jeremiah Camara was on Michael Baisden talking about his book, *Holy Lockdown*. We got excited because we were like finally! Someone else was calling out the Black Church for what it is and how it really has not done much to help our communities. But when *Religulous* came out, I started trying to get a better understanding because I was one of those people who said "agnostic" because it was a "safe word." To actually say "atheist," even up until a couple of months ago, I was still struggling with that. But I finally had to go, "You know what, I don't believe. At All." And it's not because I'm angry with anybody. It's because I just don't believe. I never have believed. I just don't.

I remember paying close attention to mythology when I was in elementary school. So, I was very aware that there were other countries that had a god concept. I remember asking myself the question, "Why is the Christian god named 'God,' but in other cultures, 'god' is a title.

What is so special about the Christian god?" I was like, "Huh? That doesn't make any sense." I remember discussing the story of Horus, Isis, and Osiris and how Seth killed Osiris, but Isis was able to impregnate herself through the immaculate conception. I didn't really put two-and-two together about it being similar to Jesus until I was an adult. And of course, I was already raised with the belief that a lot of Eurocentric ideas were plagiarized and borrowed from a lot of African traditions, especially from Egypt. But as far as the religious aspect of it, it didn't really hit me that the Jesus concept was borrowed from other religions until I was older. And now when I think about it, that indoctrinated fear is so powerful. People will question everything else except their belief in god. They know it doesn't make any sense. They know there are other cultures that have gods, but they are afraid to say that it isn't real.

So, for me to come to realization and say, "You know what? Yes, I am an atheist," was not hard for me because, as I said, I was never fully indoctrinated into the god concept, which was something I was very thankful for.

Coming Out. . . Completely
"And if you would've told me a year ago, or a month ago, that this would be in the direction that I'm in now. . . . I would've said you were lying."

Mandisa says that many of her family members know what she is an atheist, but that she tries not to broadcast it around them out of respect for them, especially when she is in their homes. Though her atheism hasn't had a profound effect on her relationship with her extended family, she is more excited about the growing number of black atheists and nonbelievers who are coming out to form a strong community.

Some of my family know that I'm an atheist. The ones that are on Facebook know. I don't think that my grandmother knows. Someone may have told her but I just try to respect her wishes. So when she says, "Oh, the lord woke me up." I just say "mmm-hmmm." I'm not one of those people who will say, "Grandma, I'm an atheist. So, I don't believe what you believe." It's interesting because one of my cousins recently married a preacher. So now she's this first lady and tries to act smart. She actually called into question why the church was so stagnant. And I wanted to say to her, "It's because your beliefs are stagnant. You're looking at a 2,000-year-old book that you've been told you had to read all your life. You're looking at that as truth. That is the reason why you're stagnant." But then she asked me what my beliefs were and I wasn't going to lie to her. I just told her that she wasn't ready for it. But I did explain to her that I do not subscribe to a belief in a higher being and that I am an atheist.

My husband's pretty much a nonbeliever as well. I don't think he would identify himself as an atheist, but he is definitely a nonbeliever. He has pretty much always been a nonbeliever. His parents were brought up Christian. But then they stopped going to church. So, he wasn't necessarily raised to be religious. He's always been the type of person who questioned his surroundings, always a critical thinker. So, the fact that we hooked up and had the same mind-set was pretty cool.

I am in contact with a lot of people who were very strong believers and they're not anymore. Now, they're finding it very difficult to connect with other atheists and nonbelievers. So, we're trying to let people know that we are here and there are other black atheists, other humanists. And there are more people coming out; so, you are not alone in your thought process. There are others who struggle with the same things. I've had some of my high school peers actually thank me for saying the things that I do say because they've felt the same way.

Even if some of them still subscribe to a god concept, they have definitely broken away from organized religion and are becoming very skeptical. It's been really great and it helps me, too, to know that there are people like me. Some people will try to make you feel like you are alone. Like my teacher. She thinks that I'm walking down a very dangerous path. She admitted that she is afraid for the nonbeliever. But I know where that fear comes from.

And if you would've told me a year ago, or a month ago, that this would be in the direction that I'm in now, where I would be interviewed as someone who, I guess, is viewed as key to this movement, I would've said you were lying. After doing some research, I see that there are other black atheists who have been out longer and have been more vocal about it than I have. So, you couldn't have told me that I would be someone who is looked at as an inspiration in this thing. It's very interesting that this is happening. And I'm very excited that this is happening. It is past time. People really, really need to wake up. They really need to shed that fear. They really need to become more self-confident. That is what it boils down to. We really have a self-esteem problem in our communities. Most of us keep looking to something else to make us great, but we need to look within ourselves and know just how great we are as people.

Problems with the Church
"They've held on to this idea and it's crippling us."

Mandisa's critiques of the Black Church are clearly born from the heart of a proud black woman who wants to see better for her brothers and sisters. Her cultural upbringing colors her opinions about the problems facing black women, while her humanist ideals allow her to see the solutions.

They're the worst ones—black women who don't go to church on a regular basis but still believe in the Bible and Jesus. They're the most judgmental. I have had a few of my friends distance themselves from me. They didn't go to church on a regular basis, but they still subscribed to a belief in god. When I actually came out strong and we founded Black Nonbelievers of Atlanta and encouraged skepticism across the board, they cut themselves off from me. I find it very interesting that they're in your face all the time with their beliefs. They have no problem saying, "Thank god this" and "You should come to church with me." But if you're very vocal about your atheism, it's a serious problem. It's intolerable to them and they'll say that they respect your beliefs and your viewpoint, but they really don't.

As far as suffering in women, many of us have accepted this idea that black males are an endangered species. That the black man is on the verge of extinction. A lot of women buy into that. So, they're thinking that Jesus is their only true man because all of the other men in their lives have never been any good. They've held on to this idea and it's crippling us collectively. When you look into the history, how black men were being murdered, we are still in a crisis and there's no getting around that, but we cannot keep looking to this invisible, nonexistent deity or this idea to save us.

I think that the biggest problem that the church perpetuates is the idea that we're destined for worldly failure because, in order to have that glorious afterlife, you have to suffer now. The church perpetuates suffering. Even though you may be having drug or family problems or your children are being abused, it's almost as if the Black Church hides that because it's going to make your afterlife so much better. That is one of the biggest problems.

Also, it is perpetuating that hypocrisy. Like with the Eddie Long situation—we're also putting too much faith into someone to lead us somewhere. "Who's going to be our next leader? Who's going to lead us to the Promised Land?" Instead of encouraging critical thinking and self-thought, we are perpetuating the "we're all going to go down together" mentality. If one individual decides, "I'm going to elevate and better myself," he is the bad one or she is the bad one. And they are the outcast. They are ostracized because they are trying to break away and get off this sinking ship. A huge problem is that this type of dysfunction is considered normal. Staying on drugs or having the crazy uncle who might be the molester, we accept these people because they're family. And when you do that, you actually impose that onto your children. You impose that on everyone around you. And this is how we get these generational curses as a people. This is how it is being perpetuated, this continuous being at the bottom, as if we're supposed to be there. And that has to change.

I find it interesting that the people who say that they *know* there's a god who is walking with them and protecting them are some of the most fearful people. They lead some of the most unsure, most inexperienced, and fearful of lives. And for people who are so sure that god walks with them, they just have no courage whatsoever. And I find it very ironic. I see my family members and how some of them don't know what they're talking about and I shake my head because, in their world, I am the problem one because I'm the heathen. I shake my head.

15

DEBBIE'S STORY

Dueling Religions
"And we did all the church stuff that was associated with that without any issues."

Debbie is a thirty-one-year-old biracial atheist from Philadelphia. Today, she is the outreach director at the Center for Inquiry and the director of African Americans for Humanism. Debbie recalls a childhood in which her parents encouraged her naturally inquisitive personality. Whether she wanted to follow a religious path or secular one, Debbie always felt supported. With a Jewish American father and a Catholic Trinidadian mother, Debbie had a rather unique religious upbringing. However, the religiosity and indoctrination to which she was exposed didn't come from the places you might expect.

I grew up in Philadelphia in a black working-class neighborhood. Working class is a euphemism for "somewhat poor," and my family was on the poorer side. We were on welfare until I think I was about eight. My dad is Jewish. Our neighborhood used to be a Jewish neighborhood. But when I was growing up he was one of the last two white people on the block. My mom is an immigrant from Trinidad. She came to the U.S. when she was eighteen and is black. They scraped together to send the kids to Catholic school because the Philadelphia public schools were terrible. So, we went to school and were raised Catholic because my mom is Catholic. It was a black neighborhood and the church I attended was a black Catholic church. My dad was pretty secular at that point. I think that his parents weren't too happy with him at that point when he married an immigrant, black, non-Jewish woman. So, we actually didn't see them much when I was growing up.

In the Catholic school, I went through the sacraments and was baptized. But with my dad, we'd also do Hanukkah and some of the High Holy Days. I, more than my siblings, would go to synagogue with him because I liked the music and I thought the language was very interesting. And also, they had cookies. Once a year in class around Hanukkah time, my teacher would ask if I could tell the story of Hanukkah. I'd bring in a couple of things and a dreidel because there weren't other kids who had Jewish parents. We went to church on Sundays and I had to go to church in school once a month on Fridays. And we did all the church stuff that was associated with that without any issues.

The Beginning of Doubt
"Maybe god didn't exist and . . . that blew my mind."

Although Debbie's parents were not strict with the religious education of their children, Debbie still received classic Catholic indoctrination from school. But it was the incompatibility of her parents' religions that led her to start questioning at an early age.

Most of the stuff I ran into was in school and not really problems at home. So, in the sixth grade, we were starting the confirmation process. This involved a lot of preparation for the catechism where you had to sit with a priest and answer questions to make sure that you were very familiar with Catholic doctrine. You go through this question process and then the actual confirmation ceremony. They brought a bishop in and all this. We started the studying process and one of the first Friday masses we had, I was chosen to be a reader as part of the mass. And this was a great honor. I had practiced for two days the section I was supposed to read in front of the entire church. And my dad actually took off from work to come and sit in the front pew and hear me read. So, I read my piece then sat on the front pew the whole time. During the homily, the priest basically went off about how wrong Jews are. The Jews are still waiting for the return of the messiah but they are too blind to realize that the messiah has already come and he was Jesus Christ. And my dad was sitting there on the front pew.

This was the first time that I really realized that the doctrines were very different, that Catholics believe that you have to believe in Jesus, otherwise you're going to go to hell and Jews believe that the messiah hasn't come yet. And so, I felt really embarrassed that I was sitting at the front of this church while the priest was going off about how wrong the Jews are and how they don't even realize how wrong they are and my dad is sitting there on the front pew half smiling and listening to the priest. I'm thinking, *Oh my gosh! He's insulting my dad directly. Father is insulting my dad to his face!* That got me thinking.

So, we're going along in the confirmation process and it came time to choose a sponsor. The sponsor is someone you find who's Catholic and who helps guide you through the confirmation process. Someone who's sort of an inspiration, I guess. And, I didn't choose a sponsor. My teacher asked why and I said, "I'm not sure I want to go through this. Can I wait two years and go through this when I'm in eighth grade?" And she said, "No. You have to choose a sponsor now." She told me I had to choose by Monday and I remember riding my bike on the Sunday before and thinking, *What do I do?* So, I talked to my dad about this a little bit and I said to my dad, "Dad, I don't want to be Catholic anymore. I want to be Jewish." And the reason I did it that way was because I thought that I could avoid going through confirmation and still get to think about this and work it out. How did I know the Catholics were right? Maybe the Jews were right. He said, "That's great! We can talk to the rabbi. You're almost old enough to get your bat mitzvah. And so I thought I had to choose between getting confirmed and being catholic forever and ever and ever or getting a bat mitzvah and being Jewish forever and ever and ever. And I had no choice besides that. And it was a huge decision.

So, I'm riding my bike this Sunday and I parked against the fence. I'm thinking I have to choose either the Jewish god or the Catholic god.

The Jewish god, to me, was this Moses, bearded figure in the clouds. And the Catholic god was more like sunbeams coming through the clouds. The Jews think the messiah hasn't come yet because there are prophecies that haven't been fulfilled yet. And the Catholics think that Jesus was the messiah. And what does the mean for all the non-Catholics? Were they going to burn in hell? This was very personal to me. And the Jews think they're the chosen people. Then, I thought about the Hindus and the blue-skinned elephant-based god but that was about it. And there was also a mosque beside my neighborhood convenience store and I thought to myself, *They don't even believe in god! They believe in Allah! What if they're right? How do I know? How do I know who's right?* Then it came to me. It had never been presented to me. It just struck me that maybe neither one of these groups was right. Maybe god didn't exist and that's why there are so many different kinds of stories. And that blew my mind. Sometimes people talk about an eye-opening experience. I feel like I blinked then and when I opened my eyes the world was a different place. I looked around and I was like, *There's no god in the tree. There's no god in the sidewalk. There's no god in the sky. Wow! That makes so much sense! And that's why there are so many stories. Wow! I must be the first person to ever think this.* I was so excited by this idea that I randomly came up with. I was a little naive. I didn't have any friends at the time and there was no Internet.

The next day in school, Sister asked me if I had chosen a sponsor and I said to her, very earnestly, "Sister, I don't think there is a god!" And, in my mind, she was going to be amazed by this idea like "WOW! I've never thought of that." Then, I imaged she would take it back to the convent and the nuns would discuss it over dinner and they would be very interested. And "WOW! We've never thought about this." And they might be a little confused and perplexed so they would take it to the priest and the fathers would get together and they would consult on it. And it would be this big thing. Now, I can't believe I even thought that. Sixth grade isn't that young! I just had had no idea that this idea was even possible.

And so, she flipped out. She said, "What? You listen to me, young lady, you're getting confirmed!" And I got in trouble. I remember having to sit in this room for a day and being given homework and a Bible and reading through all the Bible stories like they're all Greek mythology stories. "Oh wow! *The son of Solomon.* That doesn't even make sense. And oh, look at this with Noah and the ark. These are the same kinds of stories. They're just parables and stories and they teach us a lesson. Ahhh! This all makes sense to me now."

Sister was, of course, not happy and she assigned me a sponsor, the school secretary, who was mean. I said to my mom, "Mom. She's trying to force me to go through confirmation anyway and I don't want to make that promise to be Catholic forever and ever and ever because I don't think there's a god anymore!" My mom wasn't as Catholic as I'd assumed she was. She basically said, "Debbie, if you don't believe in god then you're not making a promise to anyone to be Catholic forever and ever. So, just go through it so you don't get in trouble." And I was like, "Oh right! I'm not lying to god because there is no god! Oh right!" I never had thought about that. And it's funny how ingrained I was in this one mind-set.

So, we went through this confirmation thing. The bishop was at the front of the church and he asked questions like, "Do you believe in the one true Catholic god?" And my sponsor's hand was on my shoulder and I said, "No." The bishop was eighty-nine and half deaf. He didn't even notice. And I was terrified about this, but I felt it was the right thing to do. And he just blessed me with oil and said, "Okay, go on." My sponsor, however, heard me and on the way back to the pews she leaned and said, "We'll talk about this later!" And that terrified me. So, I avoided her as much as I could for the next couple of years.

Two years later, however, in eighth grade, two things happened. Very early on in our religion book the words *atheist* and *agnostic* were defined. That's the first time I knew that anyone else had thought this, that god might not exist. And I underlined *atheist* like, "Oh my gosh! There's a word for this." I didn't even know how to pronounce it. I had to look it up in the dictionary. Later on in the year, I applied to go to a private Catholic all-girls school which my sister had gone to. And there was this expectation that I'd go too. It was a little pricey and I could only go if I got a scholarship by taking this entrance exam and doing really well on it. And I did. They informed my school first and my teacher announced it and congratulated me. And I got paged to come down to the office a little while later.

Now, I'm riding this cloud that they're going to congratulate me. No! Sister, still the school secretary, says, "I know you got a scholarship and I know your family can't afford to send you without that. But I remember what you said at confirmation. I know you're not going to church anymore and I'm going to tell them." And I said, "What? No! I'm still going to church, the one in my neighborhood." I lied. I had stopped going to the church. And so, she said, "Oh yeah? Bring me a letter from the bishop that says you go there." So I said, "He never sees me. I sit at the back. I go! I go!"

So after that, I ended up going to church every freaking Sunday for the rest of the school year just so that Sister could see me there. This was four miles away and involved me taking a bus and going way out of my way to go to church so Sister would not report it. I don't think I told my mom about that happening because our family's one big fear was, *Don't threaten them when it comes to them giving you money. We don't have the money to pay for it and if you screw up, you're going to go to public school.* Going to public school was the biggest threat to me.

High School
"If we ran into Klingons and Vulcans on another planet, will they have souls?"

Despite her close call in middle school in which her atheism almost cost her a private-school scholarship, Debbie could not help but ask all the wrong questions.

Then I went to Catholic high school and I started a philosophy club. My mom would sometimes call me The Questioning One. I didn't really know anything about philosophy, but I had some fun questions that we talked about. *If we ran into Klingons and Vulcans on another planet, will they have souls? If they die, will they go to heaven or hell since there's no Jesus or Catholicism?* I was a bit of a Star Trek fan. *What should the relationship be between legality and morality? Should everything that's immoral be illegal? And is everything that's illegal therefore immoral?* I was really pleased with myself for coming up with these questions. So, we met once a week all throughout the school year.

We usually had six to ten people coming to these fun discussions after school on Fridays. My sophomore year is when I started getting in trouble in my religion class. The first two quarters were focused on church history and I got As. There was no problem. The second two quarters were focused on what was called the Sacraments. There were these kinds of questions like, "God is: (A) Love, (B) Faith, (C) Hope, (D) All of the above." I had to write a lot of essays. And I was not getting As. I did poorly because I was answering them sort of truthfully. And my teachers saw me as a bit of a troublemaker even though I was quiet, and shy, and unassuming. On Fridays, different students would be assigned to bring in different things for us to meditate on at the beginning of class. One girl brought in John Lennon's "Imagine," and she said, "I like to think of this as a prayer," and she plays it. I was a huge Beatles fan and after we finished meditating on it, I raised my hand and said, "Well, actually, John Lennon didn't believe in god. That's what he means when he says 'Imagine no religion. It's easy if you try.' He's actually pro *no* religion and a socialist. In that context, it's really not like a prayer at all." Someone else brought in "Let it Be." You know, "When I find myself in trouble, Mother Mary comes to me." The student who brought it in said, "Here's Paul praying to Mary, the mother of god, whenever he's in trouble." Then I raised my hand and said, "Actually, Paul McCartney's mother's name is Mary. So, he was really talking about his mom." I was not trying to be a smart ass, but this person was very wrong and I had to correct it because I was such a huge Beatles fan.

So, the straw-that-broke-the-camel's-back paper in that religion class was a four-page assignment paper about a priestly person. A priestly person is someone who takes Catholic values and sort of ministers to the masses in some way, the same way that a priest ministers to congregations. Some ended up picking people like Gandhi, Martin Luther King, Jr., Pope John Paul II, Peter. Someone said, "my grandfather." A lot of people picked a parish priest. And I picked Bob Dylan. I justified it.

I was honest and serious. I was not trying to make a mockery of the assignment. I was really into the music of the 60s and 70s and I thought of Bob Dylan because he made positive social changes with his music. I looked it up. I used three books for my bibliography. My paper was seven pages. I used the phrase "agent of social change" multiple times. And the things I focused on were his early-60s protest songs, like "Blowing in the Wind" and then the song "Hurricane," which directly led to Rubin Carter being released from prison after having been wrongly accused of a murder. I was like, *Look at all this change he made!* Because he was a popular musician, all of this stuff played on the radio and made people think about these issues like war and other things, agent of social change. So, I was serious. And the day that the papers are supposed to be handed back, my teacher called me out in the hallway and yelled at me. "He was a rock musician!" And I was like, "Well, that way he was able to get his message out to more people!" "But he was a Jew!" And I said, "Well, actually he converted and was born again for a while. But, Gandhi wasn't Catholic. And neither was Martin Luther King." And then she stormed off down the hallway and I shook there in terror and clunked back into the classroom and everyone looked at my funny because I had just gotten yelled at in the hallway.

And she went to the disciplinarian. And the school disciplinarian's office was right there off by the room where we held our philosophy discussions. My parents got called in for a meeting. So, the school disciplinarian told them about some of the topics we had discussed in the philosophy club. They had my recent religion class paper. And they told my parents they were taking my scholarship away because it was meant for growing good young Catholic women and it was obvious that I didn't fit in that category. And I cried because I thought I'd have to go to public school and I'd never go to college now. All these terrible things. I had failed or was defeated and was embarrassed that my scholarship had been revoked and that I was going to have to leave this school. It was a really terrible rest of the year for me. But then my parents were also divorcing and we moved to the suburbs later that year and I never did really have to go to public school.

But the experience also made me get really interested in freedom of inquiry, academic freedom, and church-state separation issues. It sort of made me become a secular activist. I was really pissed off. At first I was really sad and embarrassed and ashamed. But then I became pissed off that there was a system like that and that I asked the wrong questions in philosophy club and that I wrote this really honest paper in religion class and they wouldn't even consider it because Bob Dylan was a rock musician and how could he, therefore, do good. I started another philosophy club in my next high school and I got more involved in more issues reading about church-state separation issues, and I had a real interest in that, particularly in education. My mom was mad at me with the whole losing-the-scholarship thing but the further events after that set me on the path to getting involved in the secular movement and my current job where I get to help other college and high school students do this.

College
"Yeah. Science is a white man's thing."

Hoping to go to college and to feel free to explore atheism and humanism more deeply, Debbie was surprised to find just how resistant the black college community was to freethought. The resistance came from friends who held a very Afrocentric worldview and believed that freethought stemmed from white men who wanted to tell the world how to think.

I think that in the black community, particularly, religion is tied to racial identity. If you're black and atheist, it somehow makes you less black. Being religious is tied to being black. Many people aren't too bothered if you go from being a black Christian to being a very religious Muslim. But an atheist? That's totally wrong. And that was the problem I ran into when trying to get a group together at Temple University. My black friends were not having it. Temple University is a very large, diverse campus right in the middle of North Philly. So it's very intertwined with the black community in Philadelphia. Race is an issue there. They have town hall meetings and they bring in a lot of speakers on race. They require that every student take a course that has something to do with race. And so when I was a student there, I wanted to start some kind of freethought club. Almost all of my black friends were majoring in African-American studies. They were against the idea of freethought. One of my friends who was more familiar with humanism and the history of humanism was against the idea of getting involved in a humanist group because of its Eurocentric history.

He believed the idea was, *Look at all these ideas that these white guys during the Enlightenment came up with. Now, if only we can force the rest of the world to follow this.* He had a lot of good-sounding arguments and I would try to argue. "Okay, I understand your point. How can you say one culture's better than another one. I understand the Eurocentric history but what about female genital mutilation? Can you say that that's just fine because it's just one culture's way of doing something? What about the oppression of women? Isn't there a way to evaluate these things across culture?" And he said that if we look at African societies before the Europeans got there and screwed everything up, the people were happier. They lived in harmony with nature. It was often a situation where one man had multiple wives but that worked and it would be good to go back to that. I hadn't heard him say that before and it floored me. It's fine to do it but one woman should be able to have multiple husbands, too. And he said, "Well, that's not in line with biology." And I was like, "Well, what the hell! Treating cancer is not in line with biology but we still do it." He just had no connection with freethought culturally.

Secularism in government is the best kind of government for freedom. Science helps give us the tools to know what's true about the world. I wasn't even into the history of freethought as much as I was into the freethought movement as being one of the best vehicles to achieve the kind of social change that I wanted to see happen. For example, when it comes to being pro-choice, a lot of times people get hung up on the religious belief that something that was just conceived had a soul and you're therefore killing it. Well, I thought that if you could just address the issue of the soul, if they didn't believe in a soul, you wouldn't have that argument. Or like same-sex marriage and gay rights, for which I was a big activist. When people say, "That's wrong," why is it wrong? Either it makes them feel icky or they think it's sinful. If that's the case, then we should argue about why they think it's sinful. That's an effective way to make the broad sorts of changes that I wanted to see happen. And that's what I was concerned with. And yes, when we retell the history of the movement, it's been very European. And it's always chafed me, too. But still the values at the end of the road—the academic freedom, the freedom of inquiry, the reason-based thinking, promoting critical thinking and no questions off limits, and trying to help people get rid of religion, because religion, I thought, was a harmful way of thinking that impeded people's ability to think critically about things. And so I thought I should fight against it and my black friends weren't having it.

Biggest Problem
"I want to see people held in high esteem because they're damn-good thinkers—not just because they're very religious."

Although Debbie never officially belonged to a black church, her work in the humanist movement and interest in civil rights issues has kept her in close contact with the black religious community.

I think that often we have relatively well-off white men involved in the movement who really aren't interested in volunteering at soup kitchens or collecting cans for canned food drives. They're really interested in donating to science museums and that's great but they're disconnected from the kind of social justice issues that I think a lot of black churches are involved in.

But before I go ripping on the Black Church, I would like to say one or two nice things about it. One is the interest in social justice issues but in some areas, when people leave the church, they don't have an easy social or cultural group to plug in to. It seems to me that particularly with middle-aged women, the church can be a very consuming force. On the other hand, I feel there is this sort of anti-intellectualism. There are discussions about things like social justice issues or war but there's not the sorts of values . . . I want to see people held in high esteem because they're damn-good thinkers—not just because they're very religious. And so, there are a lot of cover-ups and almost worship of the pastor. The pastor will be almost deified. Like Eddie Long. Eddie Long can do no wrong. And that's B.S. And I know that that's a human tendency and it happens in lots of different organizations, but I guess I feel like it's more poignant in the black churches.

And reinforcement of certain sex roles and gender roles is a problem. Maybe if I researched this I might find some exceptions, but black churches almost never get involved in LGBTQ issues. Never. And so, since I was always so interested in that as a civil rights issue, there was almost always *no* support for that from the black community. While we might get some support from some of the liberal churches for LGBTQ stuff, in the Black Church, it's very much like, *This is how to be a man. This is how to be a woman.* Men are generally the preachers and women are generally the volunteers doing all the work. Generally speaking, those are some of the things that I think are out there that are reinforcing some of the cultural values that I don't think are the best.

16

ON MOVING FORWARD

"To be truly visionary we have to root our imagination in our concrete reality while simultaneously imagining possibilities beyond that reality."
—bell hooks

In any field, on any topic, in any group of people, it is important that critics put forth meaningful solutions to the problems they highlight. I do not intend that this list of suggestions be exhaustive. The problems facing black women are many and will not be solved through the prescriptions of one book. But as is often the case, personal change occurs through private reflection and social change occurs through organized, communal efforts, one person at a time.

The Importance of Questioning
"I feel I now look at the world not as a child, but as an adult. . . . I also see what is beautiful, what is wonderful."
—Julia Sweeney

Obviously, I want to promote freethought. Since I believe that religion, in general, is oppressive, it should come as no surprise that I want people to be free. But I would never force anything on a person. With that said, I believe that the first and most important step of all is for black women to take the time to read and research the details of Christianity. Just as I do not want them to take the words and rules of the church at face value, I also do not want them to take nonbelievers' criticisms as completely true either. Unfortunately, many Christians have not read the entire Bible. If a person is going to hold herself to a set of religious rules, laws, and expectations, she should at least independently study the religion she's adhering to, even if on the most basic level. I suggest that women make a list of questions about Christianity, Jesus, the Bible, or other aspects of religion and then seek answers to those questions—not just from her preacher or minister, but from independent sources.

Perhaps one may have general questions about the Bible or specific questions about Jesus. Or maybe a person wants to know the history of a certain word because the Bible has so many translations. Performing basic research and dissecting the meanings of various key words and phrases can be very enlightening. Take the word "hell," for example. There are four Greek and Hebrew words—sheol, hades, tartarus, and gehenna— that are all translated as "hell," but each offers vastly differing spiritual implications based on their orginial meaning. Two good resources for examining translation issues are the Blue Letter Bible Web site (www. BlueLetterBible.org) and *Strong's Exhaustive Concordance of the Bible*. Asking questions is a good thing. When people tell us that being curious is a bad thing, it is often because they have something to hide. So it is with religion.

Another suggestion I have is for women to create a list of their personal values about life, love, relationships, family, and other important topics and then study what the Bible has to say about them. Examine how god and Jesus respond to various scenarios. If you find information that does not sit well with you, research it more. Maybe you value a woman's right to control her own body and life. Ask what the Bible has to say about a woman's right to self-actualization. But whatever you do, if you find something that you believe is immoral or diametrically opposed to your own conscience, avoid the mental gymnastics and cognitive distortions needed to excuse the inexcusable. Most people value things like freedom and honesty. Our society values our children. We value peace and nonviolence. Research what the Bible actually says, not what preachers or ministers say, about these topics and analyze the stories of the Old and New Testaments to learn more about the nature of the Christian god.

The Benefit of Personal Reflection

"It's a violation almost immoral in its transgressiveness to shirk the responsibilities of rationality."
—*Rebecca Newberger Goldstein*

For personal reflection, I suggest that black women who are questioning their beliefs or who are simply interested in learning more about nonbelief first make attempts to get to know other nonreligious people of any race or sex, but especially nonreligious black women. As Peter Paris notes,

> Regardless of the measure of success that betrayers of the black Christian tradition may achieve, they have never been able to gain full legitimacy within the black community. Those who compromise the tradition are received, at best, ambivalently, and, at worse, they become liable to the community's most opprobrious epithet, "Uncle Tom." Those who explicitly attack the tradition alienate themselves from the community.[1]

This is why it is important for believers to get to know people who hold different beliefs from their own. It is an essential step in decreasing one's anxiety about "those people" and increasing one's understanding of others' world views. This sort of act helps a person be more tolerant, respectful, and socially conscious. This truth has been born out in many changes throughout history from the Civil Rights Movement to our understanding of mental illnesses, from gay rights to learning disabilities. If you don't know any nonreligious women, go to Facebook and make friends with women from any number of black atheist, agnostic, humanist, and secular groups. You will find that most nonreligious people are more than willing to talk about religious topics with you as long as you show genuine interest in what they have to say and are not there to be an Internet "troll" or to proselytize. You know plenty about your religion and chances are that the black nonbelievers you meet will also know lots about Christianity. What you should try to do is learn about another person's point of view.

I also suggest that black women take stock of their own emotional needs. Taking the Patient Health Questionnaire–9 (PHQ-9) for depression and the Generalized Anxiety Disorder Scale–7 (GAD-7) found in the appendix are a good place to start. If you get significant scores, do something about it. If you have insurance, go to the doctor or see a counselor. If you do not have insurance, go to a community health center. If you do not have access to any medical resources, make an earnest effort to incorporate into your life activities that are shown to alleviate depression and anxiety symptoms such as exercising. If you feel isolated and alone, try to find a group of women who will make you feel supported. There are all kinds of personal and social activities that can lead to increased emotional health. However, it is important to appreciate the fact that, for some people, depression, anxiety, and other mental illnesses have true biological, neurological, and hormonal bases for which medical treatment is the primary and most effective way to alleviate symptoms.

The Role of Science

"Do whatever it takes to not fool yourself. Period.
That's the scientific method."
—*Neil deGrasse Tyson*

Black humanists, atheists, and secularists frequently point out that, among black nonbelievers, scientific research and study is usually a low priority. They highlight that black nonbelievers often focus on issues of social justice and racism. I believe that those goals and scientific study do not have to be mutually exclusive. In the black community, many people accuse atheism and skepticism of being something that only white men care about. While the Enlightenment and freethought movements have largely seen white men at the forefront, that is no excuse to ignore such a potentially meaningful part of one's education. Science proficiency in the United States is consistently and significantly lower than in many nations in the developed world. In nations and communities where there is a strong appreciation of the sciences, harmful superstitions are conspicuously absent from society. Indeed, the vast majority of scientists profess to be atheists, agnostic, or nonbelievers of some kind.

I suggest that black people—nonbelievers and believers alike—take a stronger interest in the sciences. For the believer, gaining even a cursory understanding of evolution or cosmology can give her something concrete to which she can compare her supernatural beliefs. One excellent resource is Neil deGrasse Tyson's radio show, *StarTalk Radio*. The shows are archived on iTunes podcasts and at www.StarTalkRadio.net. These shows cover a wide range of topics in an easily accessible, understandable, and entertaining way so that those new to such concepts will not feel threatened.

When faced with the strong evidence for the truth of evolution, for example, it is hard to continue to hold on to creationist beliefs. For the woman who has already given up her supernatural beliefs, a deeper understanding of the natural world can help her solidify her reasons for her nonbelief. Having something more than emotional or psychological reasons for giving up religion gives a woman a stronger ground to stand on during the times when she may be tempted to return to religion. It is not unusual for ex-believers to go through fleeting moments in which they doubt their reasons for doubting. But being sure within oneself about the case for becoming a nonbeliever and one's knowledge base can be comforting.

I also think that it is important for black women to take a greater interest in science so that she can spread her critical and skeptical thinking to others. This is especially true if she has kids. As a woman who has given up her supernatural beliefs, I believe it is of the utmost importance to instill in my daughter the ability to think critically about the world. I want her to be a freethinker and avoid harmful indoctrination. I can trust that my daughter will make rational choices throughout her life if I know that she is a critical thinker. As they say, the children are the future and, if we are hoping for a brighter future, we must help our children become more adept at evaluating the world around them.

The Growing Community
"My hands went out automatically to touch theirs, reaffirming the reality that we are all in this together."
—Alice Walker

Throughout the interviews, one thing that became obvious was that many of the women came to change their religious beliefs through self-reflection and research. And they quickly found the need to build new support systems. Groups and organizations are starting to spring up in order to address the social, emotional, cultural, and even political needs of the scores of black men and women who are discovering and becoming vocal about their nonbelief. There are hundreds of Meetup.com groups dedicated to atheists and dozens that explicitly offer activities for black atheists, humanists, and nonbelievers. There are scores of Facebook groups for black nonbelievers. There are even national organizations and nonprofits such as Black Atheists of America and African Americans for Humanism that are appearing on the national stage to increase the visibility of this small but growing section of society. A section of hip hop is even being carved out by acts like Greydon Square that explicitly speak to black atheists and nonbelievers. Not only do these groups build a sort of collective voice as a way to represent many still-hidden atheists, but they also serve as hubs for information and guidance to those who are considering leaving behind their superstitions, or searching for others with whom they can connect.

As black women start to have concerns about their beliefs, I cannot emphasize enough the importance of not simply asking questions but also seeking out unbiased answers to them. In order for black women to continue to improve their lots in life, it is going to be essential that we start to take responsibility for our own thoughts, feelings, and behaviors and make changes where we see the need. We should no longer pawn off our worries and insecurities on an unseen entity that we hope will change things for us. We should no longer blame so-called evil forces for the things that go wrong in our lives. We are beyond suffering in silence. Black women who embrace freethought and skepticism will find themselves shedding the harmful ideology of Christianity. Black women who embrace humanism will find themselves with a superior moral system to the judgmental, critical, and close-minded morality of the Bible. Black women who embrace atheism and agnosticism will find themselves free of constant fear of sin and hell. It should now be clear that the nonreligious black woman is not any more or less intelligent than the religious one. No. She has simply shed her superstitious past and instead embraced a future full of light, hope, and freedom.

GENERALIZED ANXIETY DISORDER-7

GAD-7

Over the last 2 weeks, how often have you been bothered by the following problems? (Use "✔" to indicate your answer)	Not at all	Several days	More than half the days	Nearly every day
1. Feeling nervous, anxious or on edge	0	1	2	3
2. Not being able to stop or control worrying	0	1	2	3
3. Worrying too much about different things	0	1	2	3
4. Trouble relaxing	0	1	2	3
5. Being so restless that it is hard to sit still	0	1	2	3
6. Becoming easily annoyed or irritable	0	1	2	3
7. Feeling afraid as if something awful might happen	0	1	2	3

(For office coding: Total Score T____ = ____ + ____ + ____)

Developed by Drs. Robert L. Spitzer, Janet B.W. Williams, Kurt Kroenke and colleagues, with an educational grant from Pfizer Inc. No permission required to reproduce, translate, display or distribute.

GAD-7 Scoring Instructions

The Generalized Anxiety Disorder–7 Anxiety Inventory consists of seven items that can be scored on a range of 0 to 3. To find your score, add your ratings from each of the seven items together. A score of 10 or greater is recommended for further evaluation.

- 0–5, None to nominal
- 5–9, Mild anxiety
- 10–14, Moderate anxiety
- 15–21, Severe anxiety

PATIENT HEALTH QUESTIONNAIRE-9

PATIENT HEALTH QUESTIONNAIRE-9 (PHQ-9)

Over the last 2 weeks, how often have you been bothered by any of the following problems? (Use "✔" to indicate your answer)	Not at all	Several days	More than half the days	Nearly every day
1. Little interest or pleasure in doing things	0	1	2	3
2. Feeling down, depressed, or hopeless	0	1	2	3
3. Trouble falling or staying asleep, or sleeping too much	0	1	2	3
4. Feeling tired or having little energy	0	1	2	3
5. Poor appetite or overeating	0	1	2	3
6. Feeling bad about yourself — or that you are a failure or have let yourself or your family down	0	1	2	3
7. Trouble concentrating on things, such as reading the newspaper or watching television	0	1	2	3
8. Moving or speaking so slowly that other people could have noticed? Or the opposite — being so fidgety or restless that you have been moving around a lot more than usual	0	1	2	3
9. Thoughts that you would be better off dead or of hurting yourself in some way	0	1	2	3

FOR OFFICE CODING ___0___ + _____ + _____ + _____

=Total Score: _____

If you checked off any problems, how difficult have these problems made it for you to do your work, take care of things at home, or get along with other people?

Not difficult at all	Somewhat difficult	Very difficult	Extremely difficult
☐	☐	☐	☐

Developed by Drs. Robert L. Spitzer, Janet B.W. Williams, Kurt Kroenke and colleagues, with an educational grant from Pfizer Inc. No permission required to reproduce, translate, display or distribute.

PHQ-9 Scoring Instructions

The Patient Health Questionnaire–9 Inventory consists of nine items that can be scored on a range of 1 to 3. To find your score, add your ratings from each of the seven items together. For a score in the 10–14 range, consideration of counseling or medications is recommended. For scores of 15 and above, active counseling and medications are recommended.

- 0–5, None to nominal
- 6–9 , Mild depression
- 10–14, Moderate depression
- 15–19, Moderately severe depression
- 20–27, Severe depression

APPENDIX 3

THINKING PATTERNS INVENTORY

For the following items, think about how much you agree with the statements. Rate each statement on a scale from 0 to 6, with 0 meaning that you completely disagree with the statement and 6 meaning that you completely agree with it.

0. *Complete Disagree*
1. *Mostly Disagree*
2. *Somewhat Disagree*
3. *Partly Agree and Partly Disagree*
4. *Somewhat Agree*
5. *Mostly Agree*
6. *Completely Agree*

1. _____ I don't have to consider the specifics of a situation to know if something is right or wrong, good or bad.

2. _____ I'm always prepared for the worst.

3. _____ I don't usually feel safe.

4. _____ I'm not really good at anything.

5. _____ There are always signs of when something bad is going to happen.

6. _____ When I make a mistake, people blow it out of proportion when it really isn't a big deal.

7. _____ I am not a very smart person.

8. _____ I am useless if I make a mistake.

9. _____ I always mess things up.

10. _____ If people didn't bother me, I wouldn't have any problems.

11. _____ Showing your feelings can get you into trouble. So, I have to hide mine.

12. _____ I can be a mean person.

13. _____ Most problems have only one right answer.

14. _____ I can't think of the last time I did something really good.

15. _____ The world is a scary place.

16. _____ No one notices when I do something good.

17. _____When I'm having a bad day, I think "What's the point?"

18. _____ It is awful if people don't like me.

19. _____ I always get a sense of when something bad is going to happen.

20. _____ Bad things always seem to happen to me.

21. _____ I'm a good person. I should get what I want.

22. _____ Sometimes I make mountains out of mole hills.

23. _____ Women can be such bitches.

24. _____ Right is right and wrong is wrong

25. _____ A small mistake can be a big deal.

26. _____ It's someone's fault (parents, spouse, child, neighbor, etc) that I am having that the problems I am.

27. _____ I know I'm a bad person because I feel like one.

28. _____ When something bad happens to me, I protect myself by preparing for it to happen again.

29. _____ If I feel really sad it's because something is wrong with me.

30. _____ I can't help being the way I am.

31. _____ I can tell a lot about people from just one meeting.

32. _____ I know that people say bad things about me behind my back.

33. _____ I can tell when people are thinking bad things about me.

34. _____ Everything should go my way.

35. _____ In order for the world to be fair, bad people must be punished.

36. _____ I'm a perfectionist. When I make one mistake, the whole thing is messed up.

37. _____ Situational ethics is just another word for letting people to get away with doing bad things.

38. _____ People push my buttons.

39. _____ When I am out of shape I feel ugly.

40. _____ Nobody (or very few people) really love me.

41. _____ You can't really trust anyone in this world today.

42. _____ My life is full of pain.

43. _____ Men are dogs.

44. _____ There is so much at stake in my life I can't afford to make mistakes.

45. _____ Fair means that everyone is treated equally.

46. _____ Most stereotypes have some truth to them.

47. _____ There isn't really anything that I like about my body.

48. _____ One bad thing can ruin my day.

49. _____ If I apologize when I'm wrong, the other person is supposed to just drop it.

50. _____ I hope for the best but prepare for the worst.

Thinking Patterns Inventory Scorecard

Write the number that you selected for each item below. Each thinking domain had five corresponding statements. Once you've transferred your responses for the specific items to this sheet, add up your total score. The domains that have the highest average scores are the thinking patterns that may need to be reevaluated and adjusted.

Black-and-White Thinking

1. _____
13. _____
24. _____
37. _____
45. _____
Total _____

Discounting the Positives

4. _____
14. _____
36. _____
42. _____
47. _____
Total _____

Overgeneralizations

2. _____
28. _____
31. _____
41. _____
46. _____
Total _____

Jumping to Conclusions

5. _____
19. _____
32. _____
33. _____
50. _____
Total _____

Focusing on the Negative

3. _____
15. _____
16. _____
20. _____
48. _____
Total _____

Magnification and Minimization

6. _____
18. _____
22. _____
25. _____
49. _____
Total _____

Emotional Reasoning

8. _____

17. _____

27. _____

29. _____

40. _____

Total _____

Should Statements

11. _____

21. _____

34. _____

35. _____

44. _____

Total _____

Name-Calling

7. _____

12. _____

23. _____

39. _____

43. _____

Total _____

Blame

9. _____

10. _____

26. _____

30. _____

38. _____

Total _____

Summaries of Cognitive Distortions
in Thinking Patterns Inventory

1. Black-and-White Thinking: You look at things in absolute, good-and-bad, right-and-wrong, black-and-white categories.

2. Overgeneralizations: You come to a general conclusion based on a single incident or piece of evidence. If something bad happens once, you expect it to happen over and over again.

3. Focusing on the Negative: You only see problems, failures and wrong-doings. You only pay attention to the negatives.

4. Discounting the Positives: You insist that your accomplishments or positive qualities don't count.

5. Jumping to Conclusions: You jump to conclusions not warranted by the facts.

    a. Mind Reading: You assume that people are reacting negatively to you.
    b. Fortune-Telling: You predict that things will turn out badly.

6. Magnification and Minimization: You blow things way out of proportion or you shrink their importance.

7. Emotional Reasoning: You reason from your feelings. If you feel it, then it must be true. "I feel like an idiot, so I really must be one."

8. Should Statements: You criticize yourself or other people with "should," "shouldn'ts," "musts," "oughts," and "have to."

9. Name-Calling: Generalizing one or two qualities into a negative global judgement.

    a. Self: Instead of saying: "I made a mistake," you tell yourself, "I'm a failure" or "I'm a loser."
    b. Others: Instead of saying, "He's having a bad day," you tell yourself, "He's such a jerk!"

10. Blame: You find fault instead of solving the problem.

    a. Self-Blame: You blame yourself for everything. If something goes wrong, you take all of the blame on yourself.
    b. Other-Blame: You blame others and overlook ways you contribute to the problem.

RESOURCE GUIDE

There are some very good resources and organizations available to the unbeliever or questioner. Below is a brief listing of some of the more prominent or well-known such groups. Imbedded within many of these organizations' Web sites are often links to even more organizations, programs, and resources. Take the time to browse through all of these sites as you proceed with your personal studies.

Advocacy and Education

Center for Inquiry (CenterForInquiry.net)—Aims to foster reason and humanist values through research, education, outreach, and advocacy.

African Americans for Humanism (AAHumanism.net)—An affiliate program of the Council for Secular Humanism. It provides education and resources geared toward supporting nonbelieving African-Americans. It also links various black atheist, agnostic, and humanist groups throughout the country.

Black Atheists of America (BlackAtheistsofAmerica.org)—Seeks to provide education and support to the growing black atheist population.

Freedom from Religion Foundation (FFRF.org)—The nation's largest organization of atheists, agnostics, and freethinkers and a self-described "watchdog" of church-state issues in government.

American Atheists (Atheists.org)—Founded by Madalyn Murray O'Hair, the activist remembered for successfully having prayer removed from public schools, and is a national organization dedicated to ensuring absolute separation of church and state.

The Richard Dawkins Foundations for Reason and Science (RichardDawkins. net)—Supports science education and critical thinking to specifically combat religious fundamentalism and superstition.

The Skeptics Society (Skeptic.com)—Dedicated to investigating "extraordinary claims of all kinds" and promoting critical thinking.

The Brights (The-Brights.net)—Focuses on increasing the public's awareness and understanding of those with naturalistic worldviews free from supernatural beliefs.

Research and Study

The Skeptic's Annotated Bible (SkepticsAnnotatedBible.com)—An online resource for Bible study and research. The user can search specific topics such as "rape," "prophesy," and "contradictions" to read the exact verses in the Bible related to those topics.

The Blue Letter Bible (BlueLetterBible.org)—An online resource for Bible study and research. It is good for reading side-by-side variations and translations of the Bible as well as for seeing the verses in their original languages.

Support Groups

Recovering from Religion (RecoveringFromReligion.org)—Provides a supportive community for individuals leaving their religion.

The Clergy Project (ClergyProject.org)—Provides a supportive community specifically for former ministers or clergy who have left their faith and for those who are still working in ministry but who are keeping their newfound nonbelief a secret.

The Secular Therapist Project (SecularTherapy.org)—A place to find and connect to mental health professionals who will provide explicitly secular therapy without trying to convince you that you need spirituality to feel balanced and happy.

Reading

The list of suggested books to read would be too long to even begin to list them here. Many of the Web sites and organizations listed herein maintain sections for suggested materials.

NOTES

Introduction

1. Sikivu Hutchinson, *Moral Combat* (Los Angeles: Infidel, 2011), 36.

2. C. Eric Lincoln, as quoted in Peter J. Paris, *The Social Teachings of the Black Churches*, (Philadelphia: Fortress Press, 1985), 8.

3. Hutchinson, *Moral* Combat, 39.

4. C. Eric Lincoln and Lawrence H. Mamiya, *The Black Church and the African American Experience* (Durham: Duke University Press, 1990), 7.

5. Anthony Burnside, "From Christianity to Sanity," in *The Black Humanist Experience: An Alternative to Religion*, ed. Norm R. Allen, Jr. (Amherst: Prometheus, 2003), 124.

6. Hutchinson, *Moral Combat*, 27.

7. Ibid., 40.

8. Ibid., 39.

Chapter 1

1. Barry A. Kosmin and Ariela Keysar, *American Religious Identification Survey (ARIS 2008) Summary Report* (Hartford, CT: Institute for the Study of Secularism in Society & Culture, 2009); Pew Forum on Religion & Public Life, *U.S. Religious Landscape Survey* (Washington, DC: Pew Research Center, 2008).

2. Lincoln and Mamiya, *Black Church*, xii.

3. "Abolition," Freethought Trail, www.freethought-trail.org/profile.php?By=Cause&Page=1.

4. Hutchinson, *Moral Combat*, 74–75.

5. Ibid., 74.

6. Ibid., 74.

7. Peter J. Paris, *The Social Teaching of the Black Churches* (Philadelphia: Fortress Press, 1985), 16.

Chapter 4

1. Center for Disease Control, "Leading Causes of Death by Race/Ethnicity-All Males-United States," www.cdc.gov/men/lcod/index.htm.

2. Charisse C. Jones and Kumea Shorter-Gooden, *Shifting: The Double Lives of Black Women in America* (New York: Harper, 2003), 19.

3. Hartford Institute for Religion Research, "What's the Size of U.S. Churches?" http://hirr.hartsem.edu/research/fastfacts/fast_facts.html#sizecong (accessed June 27, 2012).

4. Jones and Shorter-Gooden, *Shifting*, 125.

5. Hutchinson, *Moral Combat*, 19.

6. Jones and Shorter-Gooden, *Shifting*, 124.

7. Mental Health America, "Depression and African Americans," www.nmha.org/index.cfm?objectid=C7DF94D0-1372-4D20-C8464F9E181D55D8 (accessed June 27, 2012).

8. A. Henry Eliassen, John Taylor, and Donald A. Lloyd, "Subjective Religiosity and Depression in the Transition to Adulthood," *Journal for the Scientific Study of Religion* 44, no. 2 (2005): 187–199.

9. Hutchinson, *Moral Combat*, 20.

10. Ibid., 36.

11. Joyce Meyer, "List of Confessions," www.joycemeyer.org/Articles/ea.aspx?article=list_of_confessions_by_joyce_meyer (accessed July 4, 2012).

12. Joyce Meyer, "How to Prevent Slipping into Depression," www.joycemeyer.org/Articles/ea.aspx?article=how_to_prevent_slipping_into_depression (accessed July 4, 2012).

13. T. D. Jakes, "Dealing with Depression," video file, www.youtube.com/watch?v=3Q8rnTto98M (accessed July 4, 2012).

Chapter 7

1. Center for Disease Control, "HIV and AIDS among African Americans Fact Sheet," www.cdc.gov/nchhstp/newsroom/docs/FastFacts-AA-FINAL508COMP.pdf.

2. As reported by L. Pan, D. A. Galuska, B. Sherry, A. S. Hunter, G. E. Rutledge, W. H. Dietz, and L. S. Balluz, "Differences in Prevalence of Obesity Among Black, White, and Hispanic Adults—United States, 2006–2008," *Morbidity and Mortality Weekly Report* 58, no. 27 (2009): 740–744.

3. Pan et al., "Prevelance of Obesity," 740–744.

4. Katherine M. Flegal, Margaret D. Carroll, Cynthia L. Ogden, and Lester R. Curtin, "Prevalence and Trends in Obesity Among US Adults, 1999–2008," *Journal of the American Medical Association* 303, no. 3 (2010): 235–241, jama.ama-assn.org (accessed January 14, 2011).

5. American Heart Association and American Stroke Association, "Statistical Fact Sheet 2012 Update: Women and Cardiovascular Disease," www.heart.org/idc/groups/heart-public/@wcm/@sop/@smd/documents/downloadable/ucm_319576.pdf (accessed October 4, 2012).

6. Rachel A. Millstein, Susan A. Carlson, Janet E. Fulton, Deborah A. Galuska, Jian Zhang, Heidi M. Blanck, and Barbara E. Ainsworth, "Relationships between Body Size Satisfaction and Weight Control Practices among US Adults," *Medscape Journal of Medicine* 10, no. 5 (2008), http://www.medscape.com/viewarticle/571959 (accessed October 4, 2012).

Chapter 10

1. Darrel W. Ray, *Sex and God: How Religion Distorts Sexuality* (Bonner Springs, KS: IPC Press, 2012), 171.

2. Ibid.

3. "Children in Single-Parent Families by Race (Percent)—2010," National Kids Count Program, http://datacenter.kidscount.org/data/acrossstates/Rankings.aspx?loct=2&by=v&order=a&ind=107&dtm=431&ch=a&tf=133 (accessed September 29, 2012).

4. Darrel Ray, "Sex and Secularism: What Happens When You Leave Religion," press release, May 15, 2011.

5. Ibid.

6. Ibid.

7. Kelly Brown Douglas, *Sexuality and the Black Church* (Maryknoll: Orbis Books, 1999), 83.

8. Ibid, 83–84.

9. Douglas, *Sexuality*, 90.

10. Ibid., 52.

11. Ibid., 72.

12. Ibid., 71.

13. Hutchinson, *Moral Combat*, 33–34.

14. Ibid., 34.

15. Ray, *Sex and God*, 202.

16. Douglas, *Sexuality*, 75.

Chapter 13

1. Norm R. Allen, Jr., ed., *The Black Humanist Experience: An Alternative to Religion* (Amherst, NY: Prometheus, 2003), 12.

2. Ray, *Sex and God*, 264.

Chapter 16

1. Paris, *The Social Teaching of the Black Churches*, 12.

SELECT BIBLIOGRAPHY

Allen, Jr., Norm R., ed. *The Black Humanist Experience: An Alternative to Religion*. Amherst: Prometheus, 2003.

Brown Douglas, Kelly. *Sexuality and the Black Church*. Maryknoll: Orbis Books, 1999.

Hutchinson, Sikivu. *Moral Combat*. Los Angeles: Infidel, 2011.

Jones, Charisse C., and Kumea Shorter-Gooden. *Shifting: The Double Lives of Black Women in America*. New York: Harper, 2003.

Lincoln, C. Eric, and Lawrence H. Mamiya. *The Black Church and the African American Experience*. Durham: Duke University Press, 1990.

Paris, Peter J. *The Social Teaching of the Black Churches*. Philadelphia: Fortress Press, 1985.

Ray, Darrel W. *Sex and God: How Religion Distorts Sexuality*. Bonner Springs: IPC Press, 2012.

INDEX

ABOUT THE AUTHOR

Candace R. M. Gorham, LPC, is a researcher, teacher, and credentialed counselor who has worked with children, adolescents, and families for more than ten years. A former evangelical minister, she holds a master's degree from Wake Forest University and is the founder of the Ebony Exodus Project (www.EbonyExodus.org). She lives in Durham, North Carolina, with her husband and daughter.

OTHER TITLES FROM PITCHSTONE

Attack of the Theocrats!:
How the Religious Right Harms Us All—and What We Can Do About It
by Sean Faircloth

Candidate Without a Prayer:
An Autobiography of a Jewish Atheist in the Bible Belt
by Herb Silverman

The Citizen Lobbyist:
A How-to Manual for Making Your Voice Heard in Government
by Amanda Knief

God Bless America:
Strange and Unusual Religious Beliefs and Practices in the United States
by Karen Stollznow

A Manual for Creating Atheists
by Peter Boghossian

PsychoBible:
Behavior, Religion & the Holy Book
by Armando Favazza, MD

What You Don't Know about Religion (but Should)
by Ryan T. Cragun

Why Are You Atheists So Angry?:
99 Things That Piss Off the Godless
by Greta Christina

Why We Believe in God(s):
A Concise Guide to the Science of Faith
by J. Anderson Thomson, Jr., MD, with Clare Aukofer